LAST MAN STANDING

ROGER MOORE

LAST MAN STANDING

TALES FROM TINSELTOWN

WITH GARETH OWEN

MICHAEL O'MARA BOOKS LIMITED

This paperback edition first published in 2018

First published in Great Britain in 2014 by
Michael O'Mara Books Limited
9 Lion Yard
Tremadoc Road
London SW4 7NQ

A CIP catalogue record for this book is available from the British Library.

Papers used by Michael O'Mara Books Limited are natural, recyclable products made
from wood grown in sustainable forests. The manufacturing processes conform to the
environmental regulations of the country of origin.

ISBN: 978-1-78243-207-4 in hardback print format
ISBN: 978-1-78243-267-8 in ebook format
ISBN: 978-1-78243-951-6 in paperback format

2 3 4 5 6 7 8 9 10

www.mombooks.com

Designed and typeset by D23

Printed and bound by CPI Group (UK) Ltd, Croydon, CR0 4YY

CONTENTS

FOREWORD

WHEN I STARTED OUT WRITING THIS TOME, I HAD THE idea of calling it *One Lucky Bastard* because that's what I feel I certainly am. But the 'b-word' was thought to be a little too risqué and wouldn't look good on the bookshop shelves, so I thought I'd better come up with another title that would describe, perhaps more accurately, what I hope you will find to be an interesting, amusing and moving collection of memories and stories about friends, colleagues and loved ones I've encountered in my eighty-odd years.

Lana Turner, whom I had the greatest pleasure of working with in Hollywood, told me her pet hatred was another actress named Linda Christian, namely because when Lana was engaged to Tyrone Power, Linda found out where he was going to stay in Rome while working on a film and booked herself into a room next to his ... and the rest was history.

Why am I telling you this? Well, a while later, Linda and Edmund Purdom – who was under contract at MGM at the same time as me – started a big affair and to complicate matters further, Linda found herself in the centre of a rather sticky situation regarding *another* past affair, this time with a wealthy industrialist who had presented her with expensive jewels and precious diamonds that his family now wanted back. Linda felt she should have some recompense for her trouble, and when the day for a changeover of cash for jewels was set, she asked me to accompany her and Edmund, feeling that because I was a fairly athletic and fit young man, I would 'scare off' any unwanted intervention.

A year or two later, I was offered a TV play with Linda, and it was quite the worst script I'd ever read. Though the stage directions made it very clear why Linda was so interested: 'In the first scene, Linda makes her entrance and her beautiful hair is held back behind her ears ...'

Scene two: 'Linda comes in with her beautiful hair and dress hanging over her shoulder and looks even more lovely than before ...'

This went on, and on. Vanity was obviously in play.

But the one thing I remember from the script was the description and explanation of death: 'When one dies one has actually just gone into another room; we know you're in there but don't have the key to get in.'

That line has always stuck in my mind, and now being one of the last men standing I'm finding that a great many of my friends are in the next room. I don't wish to be morbid, nor want to write a collection of obituaries, but I do write about quite a few of my friends in the past tense ... but don't feel depressed, dear reader, feel happy that we've had these wonderful characters in our lives, as I certainly do. Frank Sinatra used to say, 'Who's going to be left to turn the light off?'

Hopefully, it'll be me!

INTRODUCTION

DUE TO THE PHENOMENAL WORLDWIDE SUCCESS OF MY first published autobiography, *My Word is My Bond*, namely sales of two softback copies and one hardback in Burkina Faso, my publishers – poor misguided people with big hearts but short purse strings – have commissioned me to attempt to pen another pack of near truths.

By the time I deliver this manuscript I will have arrived at the ripe old age of eighty-six – I hope – four score years and six, and I'm very much reminded of dear old Bette Davis saying, 'Old age ain't no place for sissies' as my creaking knees and aching back certainly attest. But where did these eighty-six years go? Many things have happened yet they seem to have flashed by in eighty-six minutes; I must have met hundreds of thousands of people, but can I remember them all, some of them … a few? Well, I'll try.

I have always imagined that somewhere in space a recording machine has documented every word, every image, and even more terrifyingly, every thought I have been involved with. I wonder what they'd think in Heaven if they tuned in to the lascivious thoughts that crossed my mind, aged thirteen, on seeing the girls at school with gymslips tucked into their dark blue bloomers as they performed in the hall or playground during PT? I know these are hardly the ideal reflections for a future UNICEF

Ambassador and I apologize for this momentary lapse into early teenage indiscretions, but at my age these matters come to mind much more readily than others, such as what I had for breakfast this morning.

I have been very fortunate to spend most of my life in the business we call 'show'. It's always interesting, often challenging and if Lady Luck favours us, and benevolent producers take pity on us, then it's quite possible to make a living out of doing something really enjoyable. I've always maintained that any modicum of success I have savoured has been primarily down to good luck; yes, it helps if you look like a hero, if you can remember lines and if you work cheaply; but ultimately, if you're not in the right place at the right time then you could still be an eighty-six-year-old 'extra' carrying a spear in a crowd scene.

While fame, success and good fortune affect people differently, we are, of course, all equal underneath; some like to think they are more equal than others, I grant you. However, proving that beyond the glitz, glamour and flashbulbs, actors are still human, is a story that was told to me by Honor Blackman, who is perhaps most fondly remembered by Bond aficionados as the delightfully named Pussy Galore in *Goldfinger*. Honor had been attending a function in Birmingham and, prior to making her departure for the drive home, took the opportunity to powder her nose. Her friend-cum-driver was standing near the door awaiting her re-emergence when two elderly ladies exited ahead of Honor and were heard by him to say,

Number 1: 'Did you see who that was?'

Number 2: 'Yes, it was her, wasn't it? Honor Blackman.'

Number 1: 'Yeah and just think, she goes to the toilet like the rest of us!'

This marks my third literary effort, and this time I want to share with you some of the fun I've experienced with showbiz folk in my long and illustrious career, along with stories and tales that I've been told. In the pages ahead, while I would like to take the opportunity of updating you on the exciting six years since the publication of my first tome (and, perhaps most importantly for any fellow hypochondriacs, to share with you all my latest ailments, accidents and surgeries), I realize – and my wife Kristina often reminds me – that tales of my kidney stones, pacemaker, accidents and the like might not fascinate you, dear reader, as much as they do me and my doctors (my proctologist, congratulating me after the publication of my first volume, did say that he'd seen me from a whole different angle ...). Therefore I shall limit the bulk of what follows to more of a mixture of adventures and anecdotes drawn from the deepest recesses of my mind – or failing that, ones I've just made up.

What I will say is that, in between paying jobs and book tours, Kristina and I split our time between Switzerland and Monaco. I've had a home in the South of France since the 1970s, the first being in St Paul de Vence – in fact that's where I met Kristina; as neighbours we used to play tennis. Now we just watch.

It's a wonderful part of the world, and very peaceful save for the odd private jet flying over. When you think of the Côte d'Azur, images of fancy yachts, golden beaches and sun-kissed restaurant and cafe terraces where patrons take shade with a glass of something pink come to mind. The tranquillity is only ever upset by the annual invasion for the Cannes Film Festival and Monaco Grand Prix – events we happily try and dodge these days.

Today at the Film Festival there are more stars than you can shake a stick at, all grappling for publicity on the red carpet. It's not an experience I enjoy anymore and my last foray to the festival was as a guest of Tom Hanks for *The Ladykillers* premiere in 2004. That night, the festival organizers kindly arranged for a car to take us, and a PR person to guide us along the line of waiting photographers and into the Grand Auditorium. However, when we emerged after the film and our job had been done there was no such PR person to assist us, nor was there a car – there was, however, a bus to the party in Juan-les-Pins.

The story of my life – I arrive by limo and get sent home on a bus!

I should warn you that there might possibly be the odd rude word in the pages ahead, not uttered by my lips I hasten to add, but by those of other people I have associated with; and while I know the majority of broadminded readers will take it in their stride, I am conscious of receiving a letter following the publication of my earlier effort, from a lady who said she'd never read so much filth in her life and my continual mentioning of four-letter words disgusted her to the point she'd never watch one of my films again. I have to admit that the immediate halving of my fan base is something that has weighed heavily on my mind ever since.

So, *Last Man Standing*, an odd title for a book of tales from Hollywood and beyond, I grant you, but it works for me as I write these stories. Many of the folk you'll encounter in these pages have shuffled off this mortal coil now – some great stars, some legendary directors, all great friends of mine from a career that spans almost seven decades. Where did that time go? How did that happen? And where on earth does one start with a book like this …?

Well, ladies first, obviously …

CHAPTER 1

The Fun – and Feisty – Leading Ladies

W HEN I FIRST ARRIVED IN HOLLYWOOD IN 1954, reporting for duty at MGM, Grace Kelly was also under contract to the studio. I remember sitting in publicist Dore Freeman's office one morning when the door burst open, and in came Grace, fuming that she'd just seen the posters for *Green Fire* – a film she'd made with Stewart Granger – and that the studio had superimposed Grace's head onto Ava Gardner's body.

'I do not have tits like that!' she shouted

The studio liked to 'sex up' their posters, in order to sell the films, all in the very best possible taste, of course.

Dore Freeman, incidentally, told me he was invited to accompany someone to one of the 'pledge luncheons' that used to be held at Romanov's restaurant in LA. All the studio heads were there – Zukor of Paramount, Jack Warner, Zanuck from Fox etc. – and it suddenly dawned on poor Dore what was happening.

LEFT: Lana Turner as Diane de Poitiers curtsies to me, Prince Henri, in our 1955 film *Diane*. Lana was always full of surprises.

Zanuck stood up and said, 'I pledge $250,000!'

'Then I will pledge $300,000!' shouted Adolph Zukor ... and so it went on, with them all trying to outbid one another.

As they came around to Dore, he wasn't sure quite how far his $65 weekly pay cheque would stretch and, thinking on his feet, he declared, 'The same as last year!', which gained a great round of applause.

When asked about Grace Kelly, all the male directors and executives at MGM would tell you how much they fantasized about doing things only men and women can do together with her. She was unquestionably one of the most desirable women in Hollywood. William Holden and Ray Milland, two of the film world's most unrepentant lotharios, were said to be 'out of their minds' with passion for her.

I found myself seated next to Grace at dinner one evening at Hollywood hairdresser Sydney Guilaroff's house. The conversation started turning to politics, of which, as a young Brit, I knew very little, and Grace said to me, 'You know, Roosevelt sold us down the river.' I'm afraid I had no idea what she was talking about, and for some time after that I often kicked myself for not being able to continue the conversation.

Some years later, when I became a regular visitor to the South of France and she had become Princess Grace of Monaco, she invited me up to the Grimaldi family's farm retreat, Roccagele, in the hills high above Monte Carlo, and that's where I first met Prince Albert who I guess was eleven or twelve. He struck me as being a very quiet and shy young man, who took great pleasure in showing me the many animals around the farm.

Grace wasn't at all stuffy as her royal status would have entitled her to be had she wished. Far from it, she had a

ABOVE: I may not have known a great deal about US politics in the early days, but I *did* know that Grace Kelly was one of the most desirable women in Hollywood.

mischievous sense of humour, a glint of naughtiness in her eye and a great passion for limericks – especially saucy ones.

Grace was a very precious gift to Monaco, albeit for too short a time.

✦

Talking of Ava Gardner, she was one of the biggest stars in Hollywood when I arrived at MGM in the 1950s. In fact MGM's publicity department was reportedly sending out three thousand photos of Ava each week. A decade earlier, Louis B. Mayer himself had signed Ava, reportedly saying after viewing her screen test, 'She can't act. She can't talk. She's terrific!'

After a few years of fairly nondescript roles, it was her part in the 1946 film *The Killers* that really launched her as a star. The studio gave her Norma Shearer's old dressing-room suite, the largest on site, with a bedroom, bathroom, kitchen and the actual dressing room itself, lined with mirrors, light bulbs and wardrobes – it was certainly befitting of her new standing.

Ava was a very funny and pithy lady, though was, perhaps, equally well known for her sexual conquests and husbands as much as her films. She was married three times in all, to Mickey Rooney (himself an MGM contract artist when they met), Artie Shaw and Frank Sinatra; and her high-profile affairs included those with Clark Gable, Robert Taylor, George C. Scott and Robert Mitchum. In fact, legend has it that it was while filming *My Forbidden Past* in 1951 that she was first attracted to co-star Mitchum, who was himself under contract to Howard Hughes, with whom Ava had been romantically linked.

Mitchum telephoned his boss. 'Do you mind if I go to bed with Ava?' he asked.

'If you don't,' Hughes replied, 'they'll think you're a pansy.'

In her autobiography, though, Ava stated that Sinatra was the real love of her life. They'd actually met when Ava was an eighteen-year-old starlet, newly arrived in Hollywood, but, despite describing her as 'smoulderingly sexy', Frank thought she was just too young at the time. Five years later – by which time she was not only divorced from Rooney but also from her second husband, bandleader Artie Shaw – they met again and there was a huge mutual attraction. Soon after, Frank left his wife, Nancy, for her.

The whole story caused a huge scandal among the Hollywood establishment, and the scandal was happily fuelled by gossip columnists Hedda Hopper and Louella

Parsons, not to mention within the Catholic Church, and among Frank's fans. Ava was portrayed as the *femme fatale* who had stolen Frank away from his family.

Frank's career suffered both critically and commercially, but Ava used her considerable influence to get him cast in what was to be his Oscar-winning role in *From Here to Eternity* in 1953. That film, and the award that followed it, revitalized both Frank's acting and singing careers. He was soon re-established as the world's top recording artist.

During their six-year marriage, Ava became pregnant twice, but had abortions. 'MGM had all sorts of penalty clauses about their stars having babies,' she later said. Sadly, the marriage didn't last, as Ava pursued other, younger, lovers while on filming locations in Europe when Frank was working in Hollywood. It broke his heart, it really did.

In the early 1990s, Tina Sinatra, Frank's daughter from his first marriage, produced a TV movie about her father. There was obviously still a feeling of great bitterness over her parents' split, as Tina chose the most beautiful actress she could find to play Nancy but when it came to casting someone to play Ava – the greatest Hollywood beauty of all – the part went to a rather plain-looking actress.

❧

A very dear friend from my earliest acting days was Dinah Sheridan. Dinah's parents ran a photographic studio, Studio Lisa, in Welwyn, where I used to do some of my modelling work, and I'll forever remember her for giving me a lift back to London in her car after a photographic assignment – and saving me the valuable train fare. Sadly, I never had the chance to actually work with her, as in the 1950s she married John

Davis, the feared head of the Rank Organisation, and he forbade her ever to act again as, 'no wife of his should work'.

Dinah told me that on their wedding day Davis said to her, 'I can't remember if you're the third or fourth, but I'm sure you won't be the last of my wives.' It surprised few of us that she later filed for divorce – and was granted one, incredibly swiftly – on the grounds of 'cruelty'. Happily, she later returned to acting and made one of my favourite films, *The Railway Children*, for Bryan Forbes at ABPC in Elstree in 1970.

It was Lionel Jeffries who brought E. Nesbit's acclaimed book to Bryan's attention and said he'd adapted it as a screenplay; Bryan read it and said he'd love to make a film version. 'But who should we approach to direct?' he asked.

'Well, actually …' offered Lionel, 'I really rather fancied directing it myself.'

Bryan readily agreed and the result was one of the finest British films ever made.

Dinah's daughter, Jenny Hanley, followed in her footsteps as an actress and in fact became a Bond Girl in *On Her Majesty's Secret Service* with the other fella. My favourite story from Jenny's career is actually from when she co-starred with my old sparring partner Christopher Lee in *Scars of Dracula*, which at one point called for a blood-sucking bat to swoop down and remove her crucifix necklace in order that the evil Count could sink his teeth into her neck. Of course, back in 1970, there wasn't any CGI and so the bat was brought to life as a model, which was operated by two prop men who were very much an item – and extremely camp with it.

For the wide shots the bat was suspended on a wire and had to swoop down towards Jenny but the problems started when it swooped a little too low and bounced off her rather ample bosom. After a couple more 'bouncing takes' the

RIGHT AND BELOW:
My modelling days
took me from Dinah
Sheridan's parents'
photographic studio
and a selection of tank
tops to the 'hotspots'
of the British seaside.
You may not be able
to see them, but I
bet I'm covered in
goosebumps.

whole cast and crew fell about in a terrible fit of giggles.

'This prompted Sir Christopher Lee to walk on set and tell everyone they ought to take the film more seriously as, after all, Vlad the Impaler, upon whom Dracula was based, had been a real person and a little more gravitas – as befitting this noble figure – was called for,' said Jenny.

Of course, Christopher's intervention only served to make everyone start giggling further, though they eventually managed to get the take, and moved on to the close-ups.

'This meant the two prop men – who were dressed identically by the way – bringing the bat down to my eye level,' Jenny told me. 'One operated the wings and the other, with his arms wrapped around his partner, reached inside it to operate the mouth. They then started bickering about how fast the wings should move versus how fast the mouth should snap, and I fell about in a fit of uncontrollable hysterics.

'"That's far too fast on the wings, dear!" said one.

'"No it's not! You're too slow on the mouth, dear. Move it faster – and squirt the blood!" suggested the other.

'"I'm not squirting *any* blood until you get the wings at the right speed."

'"God you're *such* a bloody diva!" It was impossible to take any of it seriously, let alone look terrified as a damsel in distress,' Jenny concluded.

❧

Towards the end of my tenure as Simon Templar at ABPC Studios in Borehamwood in 1968, Hammer Films moved in on an adjacent stage with a film version of the hit West End play *The Anniversary*. It starred Hollywood *grand dame* Bette Davis, along with Sheila Hancock and James Cossins in support.

Bette Davis was a formidable actress and a formidable force in the movie business. In the 1930s, for example, she took on the Hollywood Studios, accusing them of 'slavery' and saying they only ever offered her mediocre films to star in. She wasn't to be messed with, and producers feared crossing her.

A very talented, award-winning young director named Alvin Rakoff was signed (with whom I happily worked myself the following year on *Crossplot*) to helm this new Hammer production, and the British cast were told that Miss Davis was to command their utmost respect, but they were not to approach her directly on set. Furthermore, on her first day they were given instructions to gather around and applaud the star as she made her entrance.

Within a few days it was clear Bette was not only standoffish with her co-stars but even unwilling to engage in any form of dialogue with Alvin. 'She was above taking or talking about direction of any kind,' he said.

She had the producers fire Alvin, very unceremoniously, after a week and hired in Roy Ward Baker to replace him. Shortly afterwards, the Director of Photography was fired after Miss Davis accused him of not lighting her properly, and she subsequently gave her own specific instructions on where lights should be placed.

Sheila Hancock had the dressing room next door to Miss Davis's and she was able to hear the conversations through the radiator pipes and – almost on a daily basis – heard whom Miss Davis demanded be sacked next.

A decade later, Bette Davis landed at Pinewood Studios to make *Death on the Nile* and her reputation certainly went before her. When a call was placed to production designer Peter Murton (who happily designed *The Man with the Golden*

Gun starring yours truly) saying, 'Miss Davis would like to see him', it was an ashen-faced Peter who turned to his assistant, Terry Ackland-Snow, and said, 'Terry, you've worked with Bette Davis before ...' Terry took a step backwards, wary of what his boss was going to say next, '... so be a dear and go see what she wants.'

'Well, she did ask for you, Peter,' Terry reasoned.

'Yes, but tell her I'm out looking at locations. Go on, you go.'

A nervous young Terry walked to the set and reported to the star.

'Are you Peter Murton?' she asked. Terry apologized that he wasn't and that Peter was out on location.

'They tell me he designed this set?'

'Yes, he did, Ma'am.'

'It is quite the most wonderful set I've ever been on, so please thank him.'

Terry returned to the Art Department, where his nervous boss asked, 'Well? What did she want?'

'She loves the set!' exclaimed Terry. Before he could say another word, Peter had grabbed his jacket and as he was halfway out the door he turned back to say, 'I'd best get over there in that case!'

But Bette had always been feisty – it wasn't something that came with great age or experience. In her very first film, back in 1931, Bette starred with Humphrey Bogart in *Bad Sister*. They were on set one day when someone screamed out, 'Move that broad to the other side of the room!'

Well, our Bette wasn't having any of that! 'Don't you ever call me a broad again!' she declared, deeply insulted. Alas it turned out that a 'broad' is one of the biggest lights on set and they hadn't been referring to her at all. But you can bet all the crew knew not to mess with Miss Davis!

I remember they'd just opened a new restaurant at ABPC Studios in around 1964-5 and Bette Davis, who was filming *The Nanny* at the studio, came in one lunchtime and, to my great surprise, made a beeline for my table.

'I'm Bette Davis,' she said, as though she needed any introduction, and went on to tell me how she and her daughter loved watching *The Saint* on TV. My head swelled greatly, so much so that I've not got enough hair to cover it now, and a friendship was formed.

I invited Bette to join Robert Wagner and me to the dog races at White City Stadium in west London – and she loved it. The idea of being able to dine, place bets and watch races every fifteen minutes, from our table, was like manna from heaven to Bette. She did rather well financially too. The dining room was in 'sections', with tables cordoned off from each other, and everybody was so preoccupied with looking at their racing forms, eating and placing bets that they never paid much attention to us, which I think Bette enjoyed hugely. She could be anonymous for once.

Though as sweet and scintillating a dinner guest as she was, I also saw the other side of her character when she spoke to her assistant, snapping orders and instructions as though he were some lesser breed of mortal. I certainly wouldn't have wished to get on the wrong side of her.

For as long as I can remember, rumours of an intense rivalry between Bette Davis and Joan Crawford abounded in Hollywood. I, like many others, put it down to their brilliant acting in *What Ever Happened to Baby Jane?*, but no, there seems to have been a more sinister loathing that extended beyond the screen, although both denied it.

During the filming of *Baby Jane*, Bette, the antagonist in

the movie, was said to have actually made contact – in no uncertain terms – with Crawford during fight scenes, after which medical attention and stitches were required.

It turned out that the reason for their lifelong hatred was the fact that Crawford's second husband, Franchot Tone, was revealed to be the one true love of Bette Davis's life. Davis had worked with Tone in 1935 on the film *Dangerous*. Complicating matters a bit further was Crawford's bisexuality, and her declaration that although her husband wasn't interested in Bette, she 'wouldn't mind giving her a poke'.

They constantly tried to upstage and upset one another, from making back-handed compliments at The Oscars, 'Dear Bette, what a lovely frock', said Crawford when Bette was announced the winner of the best actress award, to when gossip columnist Louella Parsons first rumoured that they might star in a film together, 'When hell freezes over,' said Bette.

Some years later, when Tone was struck down by cancer, Crawford – though by then divorced from him – took him into her New York apartment and nursed him until his death.

'Even when the poor bastard was dying, that bitch wouldn't let him go,' Bette said to the press. 'She had to monopolize him even in death.'

After Crawford died, Bette continued to rant about her. When asked why, she replied, 'Just because a person is dead, doesn't mean they've changed.'

Bette gave one of her last TV interviews to Gloria Hunniford, while she was in London to promote a new book. Gloria – quite naturally – spent the first part of the interview paying homage to the actress, her films, roles and co-stars.

Bette listened for a while before berating Gloria with,

'When are you going to ask about my book, that's the reason I'm here, isn't it?'

We've all thought it, but she said it. What a lady!

❧

Another wonderful actress and feisty lady was Lana Turner. I wrote about Lana in my autobiography, about the time in the early 1950s when she taught me how to kiss on the set of the movie *Diane*. I actually thought my technique was pretty good – I had already been married twice and hadn't had many complaints in that department – but Lana taught me the new technique of 'passion without pressure' – what a lady she was! Of course, when she came to make *Diane*, Lana was already a huge Hollywood star with lots of classic films to her name – not to mention several husbands and lovers. However, I will also forever remember her for the day she told our producer on the film, Edwin Knopf, to 'fuck off', after a seemingly trivial difference of opinion on set. In fact, Eddie was so upset that he stormed directly off the stage and into my trailer, where he was sitting, pink-eyed, when I returned a short while later.

'I've known Lana since she first walked onto this lot as a young girl,' he said to me. 'And now she speaks to me like that, in front of the whole cast and crew!'

I returned to the set and asked Lana why she'd been so rotten to Eddie who was, as everyone who knew him will attest, a lovely guy. He'd also overcome disability, leaving him with only one arm, which endeared him to everyone even more.

'Sweetheart,' she replied, matter-of-factly. 'When I first

came on this lot all the producers fucked me. So now *I'm* fucking *them.*'

In 1962, Lana was making a film at MGM British Studios in Borehamwood. It was at the time of the really dense fogs – known as pea-soupers – that used to descend over London. Lana was married to Lex Barker at the time and he was visiting her on set one day when one of these fogs came down. The production called time early to enable everyone to get home safely.

Lana and Lex left the studio in a chauffeur-driven car to head back to the Savoy Hotel in London, but a few miles down the road – at Apex Corner – the driver could barely see the front of the car, let alone anything else on the road ahead of him, and Lex, being the concerned husband he was, got out and said he would walk in front of the car until either the fog lifted or they reached the hotel.

It must be about thirteen miles from there to the Savoy, but Lex dutifully paced it out and led his wife to safety – or at least he thought so, until he went to open the door of the car and discovered it was another car all together that had somehow started following him and Lana was nowhere to be seen!

⁂

And speaking of feisty ladies, they don't come much feistier – or more fun – than Joan Collins. Some time ago in Hollywood, Joan was having a romance with Arthur Loew Jr of the cinematic dynasty (not of the *Dad's Army* dynasty, as some newspapers mistakenly reported in saying she was the girlfriend of the former Captain Mainwaring).

Anyhow, one night Joan was late for a ball in Hollywood,

ABOVE: Two Mavericks and a Dynasty. With James Garner and Joan Collins – a veritable rose between two thorns – at an LA premiere in 1983.

which she was attending with Arthur. Arthur had been brooding about her punctuality for some time, and this time he snapped, 'You are fucking boring!'

'And you are a boring fuck!' snapped Joan, without a blink.

Joan has a lovely turn of phrase, as does her sister Jackie, and I love reading their books and articles. Their father, Joe Collins, was a big theatrical agent in the 1950s and was, in fact, my wife Dorothy Squires' agent, and I got to know him well. He was a very dashing, handsome man-about-town and Elsa, his wife, was a very graceful, classically beautiful woman who believed implicitly in Joan's innocence. When

Joan announced to Elsa that she wanted to marry Maxwell Reed, the man to whom she'd lost her virginity, Elsa said, 'Darling, he's an *actor* – and a spivvy sort of actor at that.'

Maxwell Reed was six foot four and wore jackets with enormous shoulders in them, a trilby pulled down over his eyes and looked every bit the gangster. He boasted of connections in the London underworld too. But in total contrast to his large frame was his high-pitched and squeaky voice.

He had been offered a film contract with Alexander Korda in the mid-40s but was sent for voice coaching first as they wanted him to sound more like he looked – big, gruff and mean. When he returned with his squeaky shrill intact, Korda dropped him. It was then someone suggested he see a lady named Elsie who taught voice production, and she told Max that if he spoke with his chin pointing downwards, then he'd produce deep, round sounds.

I was in the Army at the time I next bumped into Max in London. He was wearing an over-sized camel-hair coat, with a script under his arm and with his chin facing downwards he said, 'Hello, old man, how are you?'

He told me – in deep, rounded tones – that he was now under contract to Sydney Box and was on his way to a script conference, and just then he lifted his hand up – along with his head – to call for a taxi … and all of a sudden his deep, rounded tones became a very high-pitched shriek again.

I digress. Joan told her mother that she planned to marry Max and Elsa said, 'But Daddy won't allow that.'

'Then I will live with him,' Joan replied, with a flourish.

Elsa told me that she never doubted it, and so, reluctantly, that's why they agreed to the marriage.

Joan told me years later that one day, Max called out from

the bathroom of the flat they'd rented, 'Joan! Have you been using my fucking mascara?'

'No, I haven't!' came the reply.

'Yes, you have!'

'How do you know?' she asked.

'Because you always spit in yours, whereas I put it under the tap!'

Sadly, the marriage was doomed from the start and ended in bitter divorce a few years later; ironically just as Joan's career was taking off and her earning power was on the up. Max demanded a hefty settlement, claiming he had 'discovered' Joan. Having now been married five times, Joan says that she's kissed enough frogs to have finally found her true prince in Percy Gibson, whom she married in 2002. They're incredibly happy together and complement one another perfectly.

Joan was aged just twenty-one when she was offered a seven-year contract with 20th Century Fox in California. Darryl F. Zanuck, the rather tiny though incredibly randy boss of the studio, had seen her in *Land of the Pharaohs*, an epic set in the land of the pyramids, in which British stalwart Jack Hawkins played Pharaoh Khufu – inspired casting!

Zanuck had a reputation for propositioning virtually every actress who crossed his path and he was struck by the image of a semi-clad Joan sporting a diamond in her navel. Sure enough, when he bumped into Joan in the corridor one day he pressed her up against the wall.

'You haven't had anyone till you've had me,' he said. 'I've got the biggest and best and I can go all night.'

Joan sensibly declined his kind invitation, though she did catch sight of what she had missed when she visited his office, as Zanuck had a life-sized mould of his manhood – in solid gold – in pride of place on his desk. I've never asked Joan whether the sight of it impressed her or otherwise, but do know that another famous Joan – Joan Crawford – was in his office on one occasion and Zanuck – gesturing to his mould – said, 'Impressive, huh?'

Without missing a beat, Joan Crawford replied, 'I've seen bigger things crawl out of cabbages.'

᪥

Zsa Zsa Gabor is perhaps better known for the number of her marriages rather than anything else, and I was once coupled with her by MGM – albeit platonically. It was the studio's habit of partnering their contract artists with each other to attend events, premieres and dinners, purely for publicity purposes. I accompanied Zsa Zsa to one such premiere, and on to dinner afterwards. She was exquisitely beautiful, if a little large in the lower rear region I felt – well, not literally felt, you understand.

At one point Zsa Zsa was married to George Sanders, he was husband number three of nine I think, but she was also having a great affair with Rubirosa (aka Mr Ever Ready). Porfirio Rubirosa was a Dominican diplomat whose reputation as a playboy far exceeded any political accomplishments and was only matched by stories of his sexual prowess. His larger-than-average penis actually inspired restaurant waiters to name the gigantic pepper mills 'Rubirosas'. Many women, and some men, have assured me he was indeed built like a stallion, and his penchant for rich women saw him marry heiresses Doris Duke and Barbara Hutton among three other wives.

George was obviously aware of something going on

between his wife and the playboy and returned home one day, just before Christmas, propped a ladder up against the bedroom window and caught the duo in mid-service. The ensuing flash of a camera bulb quite put Rubirosa off his stroke, and there was a mad scramble out of the bed as George gently descended his ladder, and let himself in through the front door to wait at the foot of the stairs.

Zsa Zsa and Rubirosa sheepishly descended.

'Merry Christmas, Zsa Zsa ... and to you, Rubi,' he said in his deliciously wonderful sardonic voice, before leaving. They divorced the following April, and Rubirosa continued his womanizing ways elsewhere.

Zsa Zsa had followed her younger sister Eva to Hollywood, and it was Eva I knew better, having worked with her in *The Last Time I Saw Paris*. I was having a cup of coffee with her in her trailer one day, between set-ups, and Bill Shanks the First Assistant Director appeared and said, 'Eva, you're in the next shot.'

'Oh my goodness,' she said, leaping up and taking off a diamond ring the size of a baseball. 'I didn't have this on in the last shot, Bill. Would you look after it for me?'

'I'll put it in my trouser pocket,' Bill suggested. 'Is it worth much?'

'About $50,000,' replied Eva.

'Oh my god!' shouted Bill. 'Someone will cut my goddamn leg off for it!'

'Don't worry, dahlin',' she replied. 'It was only two nights' hard work.'

That was the difference between her and her sister – Zsa Zsa would have said it was 'only one night's hard work'.

Eva was very down to earth and nothing really fazed her. One day, while on the road publicizing a film, Eva was staying in a fairly grand hotel suite that had an interconnecting door with her publicist's room. They were due to appear at a television studio, so the publicist knocked on said door at the designated hour, entered and stood patiently waiting for Eva in her sitting room. Moments later, Eva, having thought she heard something, walked into the room absolutely naked apart from multiple layers of jewels.

Without missing a beat she spread her arms, gave a twirl and said, 'Well, Jeffrey? How do I look?'

⁂

Shelley Winters always had a great reputation for being good fun on set. We made a film together called *That Lucky Touch* in Belgium in 1975, and late one evening in the depths of winter we were preparing for a night shoot. The set-up was that I was to be filmed hanging around outside on a window ledge and then had to go off to a field somewhere – the details escape me but it was bloody cold. Consequently, my wardrobe man had procured all manner of thermal underwear for me. At one point, Shelley walked in to my dressing room to discuss something, and noticed all my long johns and vests hanging over the chair.

'What are all those?' she asked.

'My warm underwear,' I replied.

'If it's going to be cold, then I want some as well,' she said, and picked up a selection of mine.

In the film, Shelley was playing Diana, the brassy wife of the American General (played by Lee J. Cobb) and she certainly stole every scene she was in – along with making an indelible imprint on my memory when she alighted, in character, from the General's car on our location wearing a

ABOVE: Shelley Winters eyes up my socks – after all, she'd already taken my long johns … At the Garrick Club in London for a party after filming *That Lucky Touch* in 1975, with (*front row, l to r*) Shelley, Lee J. Cobb, Susannah York; (*back row*) Jean-Pierre Cassel, Sydne Rome and Raf Vallone.

lovely, warm fur coat. Just as she stepped out of the car she flashed at us – wearing nothing underneath apart from rolls of ample flesh all held in place by my white thermals.

Shelley had a great sense of humour. One evening we were shooting in a chateau and while we were waiting for everything to be set up, Lee and half the crew – and yours truly – were playing poker. Lee was a great card enthusiast. Enter Shelley Winters, sweet-faced and innocent.

'Oh! What's this game?' she asked, in wonderment.

'Poker,' Lee replied.

'Oh, I think I played that once. May I join in?' she asked with bashful sweetness.

Lee beckoned her to pull up a chair, and within thirty minutes she'd cleaned us all out! We knew never to play with her again.

A few years later, an up-and-coming young director, no doubt still wet behind the ears, was considering Shelley for a role in a film and asked her to audition. Now, you don't ask stars of Shelley's calibre to audition: you *invite* them to lunch to *discuss* a role, but you *don't* ask them to come in and read! If anybody had suggested that to me, I'd have told them where to shove their script. But Shelley loved to work and – somewhat surprisingly to those around her – agreed to meet the director at his office and run through some lines. She duly reported, but arrived carrying an enormous bag over one shoulder.

The director gave the usual flannel about being delighted she had come in to read, and how he'd heard nothing but great things about her. He suggested they go through a scene but as Shelley sat down, she opened her bag, rummaged around in it for a bit, pulled out an Oscar statuette and put it down on the desk. Then she rummaged around again, and pulled out a second Oscar statuette.

'So,' she asked. 'Do I still need to audition?'

❧

Diana Dors was perhaps the Rank Organisation's most glamorous blonde bombshell in the 1950s and 60s – and often regarded as the British Marilyn Monroe. She told the most hilarious story of returning to her hometown of Swindon to open a local fair, where the Mayor was due to introduce her to the gathered crowds but was conscious of not messing up his welcoming speech, in which he intended to refer to Diana by her birth name of Diana Fluck. He didn't want to fluck it up, you see.

The fair was about to commence and the rather nervous dignitary took to the podium. 'Ladies and gentlemen,' he began. 'Today we are joined by a star of the big screen – and someone we are very proud to say was born in Swindon. You know her today as Diana Dors, but Swindon knows her better as – Diana Clunt!'

Diana wet herself with laughter.

Oh, and another story about Diana Dors was related to me by my old neighbour from Denham, Jess Conrad. Occasionally Jess would accompany Di to cabaret functions, as she liked to have someone to present her with a big bouquet after her act – as well as help ensure the money was paid up front. 'Always get the money when you arrive,' she told Jess, 'as afterwards you're introduced to friends, family and the champagne comes out … and everyone forgets about the business.'

Anyhow, this one particular evening they arrived at a club and were shown into the manager's office and after the usual 'Hello … what a thrill it is …' etc., the manager showed them his prized plant. Well, it wasn't so much a plant, Jess said, as a triffid-like vine, and he proudly described how rare it was, how unusual that one should survive in such a climate and so on.

'Lovely,' said Di, feigning interest. 'But shall we do the business side of the deal, darling?'

After paying the money over, the manager said his office was to be Di's dressing room and that she should come and go as she liked. There was just one small snag, which Di hadn't realized until a few minutes before she was due to go on stage: there was no en suite bathroom. Come the time that she *did* realize, in her full outfit, made-up and looking

a million dollars, she suddenly also realized that she was desperate to gain some relief, but didn't want to have to walk through the assembled crowd to go to the loo – what would that do to her big entrance a couple of minutes later?

'Well, what can we do?' asked Jess, in a panic. 'They're all standing outside the door waiting for you.'

Di looked around the room and spotted the plant. I won't go into the detail but I'm sure you know where this story is going …

'And you thought a horse could pee!' laughed Jess to me some time later.

After her cabaret, Di went back into the manager's office for a glass of champagne but there was a bit of a kerfuffle as she found the manager almost in tears, leaning over his prized plant, which was no longer growing vertically but was lying, lifeless, horizontal across the floor.

'Oh, we won't stay, Jess,' said Di matter-of-factly. 'We've got a long drive home.' And with that they made their escape – they were in hysterics all the way!

⁂

I can't resist a toilet story, if you'll forgive me for dwelling in the smallest room for a moment more, and this one involves Tallulah Bankhead, a hugely successful American actress whose fame was such that, for example, she was the first choice to play Scarlett O'Hara in *Gone with the Wind*

LEFT: Ah, dear Diana Dors, a bundle of fun and a force to be reckoned with. I look a little concerned that the moose is going to take off, while Carol Hawkins looks on, bemused.

(only for her thirty-six years to appear a few too many when the decision was made to switch from black-and-white to glorious Technicolor, and instead the role went to Vivien Leigh, a mere decade younger …).

Anyhow, fame aside, Tallulah was notorious for being mean with money and the story goes that she was in a lavatory in Hollywood and discovered there was no paper. With that she knocked on the wall of the next cubicle and pushed under a $10 bill.

'Can you split that for two fives?' she asked her neighbouring occupant.

Actually, Tallulah was deported from Britain in the early 1930s, reportedly after having worked her way through most of the boys – and many of the Masters – at Eton public school, and Scotland Yard declared her a menace.

Incidentally, when the opening night of the London musical *Gone with the Wind* (which starred June Ritchie and not Miss Bankhead, but don't let that get in the way of me telling a good story) was marred by an obnoxious young actress and a horse that relieved itself onstage, Noël Coward was in the audience and was heard to say, 'If they'd stuffed the child's head up the horse's arse, they would have solved two problems at once.' He did have such a way with words!

❦

As I started this chapter with a feisty – and fun – princess, I think it only right that I should end it with another one … And you know how I like to drop the odd royal name here and there, when I can.

I first met Princess Lilian of Sweden on a visit to Stockholm for UNICEF, my first visit to the country, in fact, and Ingvar

ABOVE: With Princess Lilian, the Duchess of Halland, a wonderful lady and a great friend.

Hjartso, my liaison and contact in Sweden, had arranged a visit to the Royal Palace. The King and Queen were away at the time, so left Princess Lilian to meet with me. I discovered that she had in fact been born in Wales and had been a model, at one point married to actor Ivan Craig. She met Prince Bertil of Sweden when she was in her twenties and they fell in love, but it was many years before they were given permission to marry. Prince Bertil's elder brother, the future King, had died very young, when his son and heir was only one year old, meaning if the reigning monarch died before the child, Carl Gustav, came of age, Bertil would have to assume the role of Prince Regent – and him being married to a commoner, and a divorcee, was not something the constitution would allow.

However, when Carl Gustav did come of age and ascended directly to the throne, he granted Bertil and Lilian permission to marry in 1976.

Princess Lilian was greatly loved by the Swedish nation and deservedly so as she had a wonderful sense of fun, as well as duty, as I discovered when we went to lunch at a restaurant in the old town. I must admit that I sat rather stiffly for the first ten minutes, until the Princess pointed at my wine glass and said, 'Will you hurry up and bloody well skol me as a lady can't drink in this country until she is skoled!'

We became firm friends, and my wife Kristina also knew Princess Lilian through her oldest friend Ewa Wretman, who was married to the great Swedish cook Tore Wretman.

BELOW: And while I'm 'princess name-dropping', with Princess Anne at a Wildlife Fund Gala in 1970.

Ewa, Tore and the Princess spent many happy times together at their holiday homes in the South of France.

Tore Wretman, by the way, became a great friend – and was another person with a fascinating backstory. He began his career in the kitchen at the age of sixteen as an apprentice at the Hotel Continental in Stockholm; he swiftly moved to positions at the Opera Bar in Stockholm and then Maxim's in Paris, where he learned all about French cuisine under legendary chef Louis Barth.

When war came Tore spent a few years in the United States where, in 1941, he signed on a Finnish cargo ship for the return trip home. However, the ship was boarded by the British fleet near Iceland and Tore was taken to the Orkney Islands then on to London until 1943, when he was finally able to return to Sweden and a job as head waiter at Operakällaren – without doubt the finest, and my favourite, restaurant in Stockholm. In 1945, aged only twenty-nine, Tore was able to buy his own restaurant and, later, went on to take over Operakällaren. He became the favoured chef of the Royal Family and, in particular, Princess Lilian.

Whenever Kristina and I were in Stockholm we would meet the Princess for tea and would also enjoy many dinners together. Sadly, the last few years of her ninety-seven-year life were complicated by illness and she was forced to withdraw from public life. We were unable to attend Princess Lilian's funeral in 2013, despite the Swedish press reporting we were there, but we were able to attend her memorial service in the September, where we all shared our many immensely happy and fond memories of our times with the Princess.

CHAPTER 2

The Pinewood Years

LONG BEFORE HOLLYWOOD BECKONED ME, I FOUND MYSELF auditioning for a film at London's Pinewood Studios. Little did I realize that it would be my home three decades later for a major TV series and seven Bond films. But before I get to that, I thought it might be an idea to start where I started – and that was at the very epicentre of the British film industry: Wardour Street in London's Soho district, though admittedly my first cartoon filler-in job was on D'Arblay Street just around the corner.

It was such an exciting experience for a cinema buff like me to walk along seeing all the familiar logos of the major film companies, including ABPC (at Film House, 142 Wardour Street), Rank (at 127), British Lion, Paramount, Hammer (at Hammer House, 113–117), Columbia, Warner-Pathé and others that were all congregated on this one magical road. Wardour Street was named after Sir Archibald Wardour, the architect of many of its buildings, though along

LEFT: With my two bodyguards on my spiritual – and literal – home turf: Pinewood Studios, where I've kept an office for over forty years.

47

with all the famous film interests it also had its share of, shall we say, more 'dubious' operators in the area and this caused the street to be known – even on the sunniest of days – as 'shady on both sides'.

It was to here that hopeful producers ventured with scripts firmly tucked under their arms, would-be directors wooed film chiefs over lunch, and some aspiring actors even attended auditions.

Many of the aforementioned companies also, at one point or another, controlled the film studios where yours truly hankered to work – Rank owned Pinewood and Denham, ABPC owned Elstree, British Lion controlled Shepperton, and Hammer were out at Bray. While there were smaller concerns at Beaconsfield, Ealing and Southall, it was the larger studios that offered the most tantalizing prizes – Pinewood being the largest of all.

In 1947 the view across the fields on the approach road to Pinewood was broken only by a cluster of tall pine trees, and then, as if from nowhere, appeared the mock-Tudor double-lodge entrance, and a friendly commissionaire. It was just like arriving at a stately home.

At that time I was a rather green twenty-year-old lieutenant serving in the Combined Services Entertainment Unit and being tested for the male lead in *The Blue Lagoon*. It marked the beginning of my long association with the studio and now aged eighty-six I am Pinewood's oldest (and longest-serving) resident, as I moved into my office there during 1970, when I began work on the TV series *The Persuaders!* and I've been paying rent ever since.

RIGHT: An early publicity shot from MGM.

British film mogul J. Arthur Rank opened his Pinewood Studios in 1936 as his dream rival to Hollywood; the final syllable of which, plus the abundance of pine trees on the 100-acre site, gave him the name. When I first turned up, the studio hadn't long reopened after being used during the war as a base for the army, RAF and Crown Film Units making documentaries. One stage was also requisitioned by the Royal Mint – some say that was the first time that Pinewood had made any money.

Just before my arrival, great filmmakers were hard at work – names such as David Lean, Michael Powell and

BELOW: With Bob Baker and Monty Berman, producers on *The Saint*. Flat feet, boys? A likely story!

Emeric Pressburger, Ronald Neame, Frank Launder and Sidney Gilliat — making some of the country's greatest films, including *Great Expectations, The Red Shoes, Oliver Twist* and *Black Narcissus.* Even as a young studio, Pinewood had an outstanding reputation.

During the war years, my two future *Saint* producers, Monty Berman and Bob Baker, were both sergeants in the Army Film Unit stationed at the studio. Being the young tearaways they undoubtedly were, they'd found a way in under the wire, and used it for coming back after late-night shenanigans in the hotspots of Iver Heath. However, one night, just before breakfast, actually, they were caught midway under the wire, and were hauled up in front of the adjutant.

'What's your story?' he asked Monty.

'Well, I missed the last bus, sir,' Monty replied, 'and had to wait for the first one this morning.'

'Why didn't you walk?'

'I have flat feet, sir, so I can't,' Monty added.

Bob was then brought in.

'Why were you back so late?'

'I missed the last bus, sir.'

'Why didn't you walk? Have you got flat feet too?'

'No, sir, but my friend Monty has ... and I couldn't leave him on his own.'

They were both stopped a week's pay.

Bob, I should add, was the first allied cameraman in the ruined Reich Chancellery after Berlin fell, and was a formidable cameraman as well as a hugely talented producer and director.

For my first screen test, I was led from the grandeur of Heatherden Hall, which formed the centre of the studio lot, through long clinical corridors across to one of the five stages – a huge, dark, soundproofed room with a smell of greasepaint, make-up and burning filters on the giant lamps. Soon it was my turn to step under the lights and in front of the cameras. Even though I didn't get the part, I was thrilled just to be there.

Later, I learned that I had been recommended as a possible 'contract artiste' for the studio's Company of Youth, more often referred to as 'the Rank Charm School'. Now unheard of in the modern industry, the studio had then established a stable of aspiring talent, producing its own stars of the future: Christopher Lee, Joan Collins, Anthony Steel, Diana Dors, Donald Sinden, Kenneth More and Petula Clark were all under contract.

Sadly, for me, it was at a time when John Davis, the much-feared company MD, was dealing with a £16 million overdraft. They consequently weren't interested in a young Roger Moore being added to the roster and ever-increasing wage bills. So while I mixed socially with my Rank contemporaries, I had to slip off to earn a crust elsewhere, but I always dreamed of returning to the wonderful film factory in the Buckinghamshire countryside.

Meanwhile, over at Shepperton Studios, where I occasionally auditioned for bit parts, Hungarian filmmaker Alexander Korda was busy building his empire, and while prudence was the watchword at Pinewood, extravagance was the order of the day at the rival studio, where the charming movie mogul began an impressive production programme: *The Third Man, The Fallen Idol, Anna Karenina, The Wooden Horse* being a few of the films I marvelled at

over in the Odeon Streatham. Korda – unlike his Methodist rival J. Arthur Rank, who was a reserved and very unlikely film industry magnate – was a great showman who loved and courted publicity. He was also an astute and talented filmmaker in his own right and made his opinions known.

Guy Hamilton, who directed two of my 007 outings, told me one of his favourite memories of Korda, when he worked as an assistant director to the great man. Korda summoned Guy one Saturday morning, together with one editor, one cameraman and one assistant art director, to view the rough cut of Emeric Pressburger's first and only solo directorial effort, *Twice Upon a Time*. It was obvious that retakes were on the cards. The three Korda brothers (Vincent, Alex and Zoltan) walked in. The lights went out and they watched in silence until the end, at which point Alex lit a cigar and addressed the assembled group.

'Boys, I could eat a tin of film trims and shit a better picture.'

Although Korda was based in Piccadilly and rarely ever visited the studios, there was always the 'threat' that he might descend at any time and in the studio restaurant a large round table in the corner was constantly reserved for him.

Just before one of his rare planned visits, studio manager Lew Thorburn had stained the wood that ran the length of the long interconnecting corridors of the main house a lovely shade of red. It really was immaculate. Korda arrived and walked partway down the corridor before turning to Lew and in his thick Hungarian accent saying, 'Lew, this corridor smells of cats' piss. Do something about it.'

One of the aforementioned great films backed by Korda, and one of my favourites, was *The Fallen Idol* directed by Carol Reed, on which Guy Hamilton was his First Assistant Director. The house used in the film, by the way, was the Spanish Embassy in Belgrave Square. One of the supporting cast members was Dora Bryan, who told me she received a call to audition at Shepperton to play the part of a prostitute. Very excited, she took the train out from Waterloo and on arriving at Shepperton Station, realized that the studio was actually a couple of miles away. So she walked across the fields, arriving rather the worse for wear.

Looking exhausted and a little flustered, but in her very

best red dress and poshest shoes, she read the lines and Mr Reed offered her the part and told her to report to the studio at eight o'clock on the Friday morning.

'What should I wear, Mr Reed?' asked Dora, wondering just how tarty he envisaged the character.

He looked her up and down and said, 'What you're wearing today is fine.'

Poor Dora! She didn't know whether to feel insulted or not!

❧

Another inimitable actress at that time was Dame Thora Hird who had, by the time Dora and I took our first steps inside a studio, been making a name for herself in films at Ealing Studios – a much smaller facility than Pinewood, but equally prolific. Dame Thora later told a wonderful tale about the mealtimes there.

Prior to the lunch break each day, one of the carpenters or electricians would usually go down to the canteen to get a copy of the typed menu for the day and bring it back to the set for the crew to place their orders. On one particular day, an electrician produced the menu which offered: fried Spam and chips, cold Spam and salad, Rissoles and a couple of other items ... only the capital 'R' on the old typewriter wasn't working correctly and instead printed as a 'P'.

'OK, then,' said the spark to the formidable canteen manageress. 'We'll have three Spam and chips, four Pissoles and chips ...'

'What did you say?' snapped the dinner lady.

'Four Pissholes ...'

'That is an R! An *R* – did you hear me?' she screamed.

'Oh, sorry,' replied our trusty spark and, without missing a beat, continued, 'We'll have three Spam and chips and four R-soles and chips, please!'

❦

All of the British studios remained busy through the 1940s, but when television became a real threat the government introduced a tax on box-office receipts, which was to be reinvested in British films. Called the Eady Levy, it helped to attract many overseas producers to the British studios, including Walt Disney and my friend Albert R. 'Cubby' Broccoli. Once here, they stayed because, quite frankly, they fell in love with our studios and technicians. That love led to millions of pounds being injected into the UK economy and employment for many, many actors and creative personnel.

As I write, Pinewood is buzzing with activity and the big news is that Disney have moved in again, but this time on a ten-year rental deal bringing with them *Star Wars*, and the first film in the new series is directed by my friend J.J. Abrams.

I say 'again' because it's not the first time Disney has set up at the studio, as back in 1952 they became the first 'renters' to move in.

Whereas back then British studios had a regular tea trolley visit the stages twice a day, part of the American way of working was to have continual refreshments on set, and Mr Disney was adamant – he wanted hot and cold running drinks all day.

Keen to avoid what he thought would be a mass daily invasion from surrounding stages, Pinewood's Managing Director Kip Herren suggested one of the old brigade of tea ladies, Margaret, would man the station and thereby, after a few days, would recognize the Disney crew, despatching any interlopers with a flea in their ear. All was well and good until one day a tall moustached gentleman in a raincoat asked Margaret for a cup of coffee.

'No you don't,' said Margaret. 'You're not on this production.'

'Oh, but I am, I assure you.'

'I don't think so. I know everyone on this set and you've not been here before,' Margaret continued, as she picked up a copy of the unit list. 'So, come on then, what's your name?'

'I'm Walt Disney,' the man replied with a big smile.

Margaret melted into a corner, but Disney was apparently delighted that his pennies were being looked after so diligently.

⚜

Disney's newest employee, J.J. Abrams, came to my aid recently (and I'm so delighted he's achieved great success since giving this old English actor a job as a British spymaster on the long-running ABC TV series *Alias*) when Lucasfilm (a division of Disney) moved into the corridor just down from my office. The next thing we knew, their part of the corridor was sealed by security doors through which access could be gained only via a swipe card. Ordinarily I wouldn't have raised an eyebrow, as different productions have all had different security arrangements over the years, but the problem in this instance is that the kitchen and gents' loo are all situated in the inaccessible part of the corridor – meaning no tea, and perhaps even no pee.

Pinewood staff shrugged their shoulders saying 'That's what

the client wanted' and didn't offer any real alternative save for using the workmen's lavvy in the other direction, which, to be honest, wasn't somewhere I'd have sent a workman – let alone an international megastar such as myself – to fill a kettle. (They've since refurbished it, I'm pleased to say.)

I dropped a line to J.J. – who was still in LA – asking if we could use the kitchen, and promising that we wouldn't spill any of the secrets of *Star Wars*. The next thing we knew, not only was access granted but an apology came from Pinewood for inconveniencing us. Ah, what it is to have friends in high places.

My book on *The Secrets of Star Wars*, meanwhile, will be in shops later in the year …

⁂

Television became hugely important to me in my career, and in the late 1940s my first, and a very handy, means of earning an extra few quid through the medium came when my agent Gordon Harbud suggested me for some assistant stage management work (as well as acting gigs) at Alexandra Palace.

In doing a little bit of research for this book and *googling* myself, a certain well-known reference website states that my first TV appearance was in 1950 for *The Drawing Room Detective*.

That's not correct, dear readers!

My first tentative steps as a TV actor were taken a full year earlier in 1949 at Alexandra Palace, more fondly known as Ally Pally. The BBC produced most of its early TV programmes at Ally Pally in north London and as such it's often referred to as being the 'birthplace of television'.

While I wasn't old enough to be there for the birth itself, back in 1935 when the Corporation leased the building, I do vaguely remember the following year as an excited nine-year-old when it started its broadcast trials; up until then our only mass entertainment was cinema or radio – one of my favourite radio shows being *Educating Archie*, which was actually a ventriloquist act. A vent act on radio – work that one out!

I saw my first TV pictures on a tiny box with a fuzzy little screen, introduced by Elizabeth Cowell with the words, 'This is direct television from Alexandra Palace …' The local baker was the only person we knew who owned a TV set and it was so exciting to gather around it waiting for the valves to warm up and seeing the picture emerge. Little did I realize that, a decade later, I would be starring in my own show on the box.

The momentous day I turned from viewing to being viewed was 27 March 1949, in a production of *The Governess* by Patrick Hamilton. It was transmitted live at 8.30 p.m., and I received the grand sum of twenty-three guineas to play the part of 'Bob Drew'. According to the BBC files I was allowed to study recently, the story all took place in Drew's house 'outside London, in the middle of the Victorian epoch'. The plot centred on the kidnapping of my sister, and I had to come into the drawing room where the police had gathered and say, 'Hello, mother! What's going forward here?' I never understood the line, and am sure viewers were equally perplexed by the Victorian turn of phrase.

Other cast members included Clive Morton, Betty Ann Davies, Joan Harben, Jean Anderson, Dorothy Gordon and Willoughby Gray, whom I vividly remember describing his interest in restoring model soldiers to me, and that he had a whole battalion of them. Almost forty years later, Willoughby starred as Dr Carl Mortner in my last Bond film, *A View to a Kill*. You can't keep a good pairing down!

Almost everything was transmitted live because TV budgets didn't extend to the luxury of recording on expensive tape or film, but thankfully we had a couple of weeks' rehearsal to get everything spot on and in this instance we all decamped to the cold and draughty Methodist Hall in Thayer Street, London. Our producer/director was Stephen Harrison, who guided us through the text and explained the various set-ups the camera would move through, stressing how careful we had to be so as not to get in its way, nor to be on the wrong set at the wrong time, as it would simply have spelled disaster for the whole production. No pressure then.

The possibility of an actor drying, a scene shift not working or a camera breakdown was something of which we were all aware, but tried not to think about. Electrical equipment wasn't anywhere near as reliable as it is today and in fact during the technical rehearsal on the morning of transmission we had to wait thirty minutes for a camera fault to be remedied. Mercifully it was all right on the night.

I unearthed a couple of interesting production memos from those BBC files. One was from Evelyn Moore's agent saying that in the *Radio Times* listing for the show, 'Miss Moore's credit should also state she is now appearing in *The Dark of the Moon* at the Lyric Hammersmith'. There's nothing like an unashamed plug for one's current project!

Another memo was from the head of programming to our producer, stating, 'Running time is 100 minutes including a one-minute opening and three-minute interval. The budget will be a maximum of £660 for one performance and should include all costs of wardrobe, design, film, sound, artists, script copyright, orchestration, transport, hospitality and photos.'

Even in the hands of the most prudent BBC accountants, I don't think £660 would go very far nowadays.

Of course, beaming into people's living rooms made you 'real characters' in the viewers' eyes, and many blurred that reality with drama. For example, one of my live TV contemporaries was Leonard Rossiter who was later – and most fondly – remembered for playing the miserly landlord Rigsby in *Rising Damp*. In one particular drama he was being examined by a doctor and, while fully trousered, had his shirt off.

'You can get dressed again now,' said the doctor and the dialogue continued while Len buttoned up his shirt and moved on to the next set-up.

Before the programme had ended word came through that somehow his mother, Mrs Rossiter in Liverpool, had been out to a phone box, got through to the BBC – which was no easy task in itself – and then miraculously to the production office to leave a message, 'Len, you never put your vest on!'

Mind you, that blurring continues today, with soap opera characters often being mistaken for the actors who portray them. Mark Eden, who played villain Alan Bradley in *Coronation Street*, was innocently doing his grocery shopping at a local supermarket when he felt a sudden searing pain across the back of his head. He turned around to see an elderly lady swinging her handbag. 'That's for what you did to Rita!' she exclaimed.

I was in great demand at the BBC and on 24 April 1950 appeared in *The House on the Square* as 'John'. In fact, there were two performances, the second (or repeat) being four days later. Again, it was all staged at Ally Pally and this time for director Harold Clayton. An hour into the first performance and an electrical breakdown on the stage meant it was time for the infamous *Potter's Wheel* interlude film to appear on TV screens, along with the words 'Please bear with us while we try to restore your programme'. There were quite a few technical breakdowns in those days and so the *Potter's Wheel* was pretty well known in its day. Thankfully this time it was only on for a minute and we were able to resume; just as well we were the consummate professionals.

Drawing Room Detective was, in fact, my third BBC drama opus, broadcast on 27 May 1950. In it, I played a part as well as performed the duties of Assistant Stage Manager (ASM) for the grand fee of fifteen guineas. It was a sort of whodunnit, hosted by Leslie Mitchell, in which viewers were invited to guess the person responsible for a crime.

With no further drama casting in the pipeline, I accepted an ASM role on a few episodes of *Lucky Dip* in June 1950, which was described as being a 'Variety Hopscotch'. I was paid less at seven guineas this time, but it only involved a couple of days' rehearsal at Lime Grove, followed by the live transmission from Ally Pally. It was actually rather fascinating to be part of a variety programme as the thirty minutes featured some regular comics – Duggie Wakefield and Archie Glen – along with a terrific line-up of guest artists including Julie Andrews, George Moon, Benny Lee, Lynette Rae, Jenny Lee, The Great Gingalee and a host of extras. There was also a new TV segment that excited BBC bosses, in which a member of the public chose a tune and Nat Allen's band in the studio had to see if they could play it … If they could rise to the challenge the lucky punter received a prize of two BBC TV show tickets of their choice.

I also lent my ASM credentials to a Caribbean Miscellany called *Bal Creole* in which Boscoe Holder – brother of

RIGHT: *The Man Who Haunted Himself* was one of the first films made at Elstree Studios under the leadership of Bryan Forbes. It's now attracted a bit of a cult following, I'm told.

Geoffrey Holder, with whom I starred in *Live and Let Die* – was brought in from New York with his steel band, which, I believe, was the first time the metal dustbin–lid–type drums had ever been seen on British screens.

Being a jobbing actor I was happy to accept anything, but when the mention of a film was made I thought I'd hit the big time. The Automobile Association (AA) made a number of training films and semi–documentaries, and I was drafted in to play a patrolman, along with my old friend Leslie Phillips. I wasn't sure it would lead to my name in lights over the entrance to the Odeon, but it was a start. The exotic location for the twenty–minute epic was a road somewhere on the outskirts of Guildford and while the crew set up the cameras behind a hedgerow on one side, I was to be found across the way, happily leaning on my motorcycle combination, dragging on a cigarette while awaiting my call to duty.

Just then, an old Austin 7 with two rather antiquated ladies in the front pulled up.

'I say, patrolman! Patrolman!' called the driver, with a rather strained upper-crust accent. It took a few moments for it to sink into my thick skull that she meant me and so in my full AA uniform, puffing on my fag, I ambled over.

'Is this the road to Guildford?' she asked.

'Guildford?' I pondered. 'Well, back there I did see a sign that had Guildford on it, but I can't remember in which direction it was pointing ...'

At that moment it obviously dawned on the old dear that there was something rather peculiar about this particular patrolman, as not only did I slouch and not salute (as a real AA man at that time would have), I was also smeared in make-up. Without taking her eyes off me, she feigned a smile, reached down with her left hand and, after a few attempts, ground the gear stick into first and kangarooed off down the road. Sixty-four years later they're probably still circling the outskirts somewhere, looking for Guildford.

Meanwhile, back at Pinewood, things were ticking over nicely with British crowd-pleaser films such as the Norman Wisdom comedies, the *Doctor* series, starring Rank's biggest star, Dirk Bogarde, and (a little later) the *Carry Ons*.

Dirk Bogarde made most of his Pinewood films with Betty Box and Ralph Thomas. Betty, his producer, was married to *Carry On* producer Peter Rogers and was one of only a couple of women who had held such a role within the film industry, while Ralph – the director – was the brother of *Carry On* director Gerald Thomas. They were often described as the 'royal family' of the studio. One of the duo's films with Bogarde was *The Wind Cannot Read*, in which he played a flying officer in World War II who fell in love with a Japanese language instructor. Not a lot of people know that Bogarde had a false tooth in his upper set of gnashers and wore it throughout all of his films, only ever removing it at night when he turned in and placed it on his bedside table. Every morning the first thing he did was slip the tooth back in.

On location, Bogarde was having terrible trouble sleeping and consequently, day by day, looked increasingly more haggard on set. Ralph Thomas was becoming concerned that his leading man was going to look anything but his best, and suggested Bogarde might take a sleeping pill. Bogarde wasn't keen on the idea, but Ralph nevertheless left a couple on his bedside table and suggested if he couldn't get off to sleep after an hour or so, he should take one.

After an hour of tossing and turning, the star finally reached over and took a pill. At three o'clock in the morning, Ralph Thomas was woken by Bogarde banging furiously on his hotel room door. The star told his director that he'd taken his advice, but after getting up to use the bathroom he had noticed that both pills were still next to the bed and, yes you've guessed it, the false tooth wasn't. The next day's schedule called for a number of close-ups of Bogarde and, understandably, panic set in. Half a dozen bottles of castor oil and a jug of disinfectant were sent up to the room ... and yes, they got their close-ups.

ABOVE: Which is your favourite, Simon Templar's Volvo P1800 coupé in *The Saint* …

However, it wasn't until 1961, when Cubby Broccoli and his new producing partner Harry Saltzman wanted to set up a series of spy adventures based on Ian Fleming's hero James Bond, that Pinewood really hit the big time. Typically, I missed out on all that fun as I didn't return to Pinewood until 1970, after hanging up my halo on *The Saint* at Elstree, when Bob Baker, Johnny Goodman and I set up a new series called *The Persuaders!*.

When Tony Curtis's name was mentioned to me by Lew Grade as being one of the three possible co-stars for the

ABOVE: ... or Brett Sinclair's Aston Martin DBS in *The Persuaders!?*

1971 series *The Persuaders!* (the other two being Glenn Ford and Rock Hudson) I was immediately grabbed by the idea. I thought Tony was a brilliant actor in films like *The Sweet Smell of Success, Trapeze, The Boston Strangler* and, of course, he showed his comedic skills in *Some Like It Hot* in which he based his English accent on Cary Grant. Incidentally, when director Billy Wilder later told Cary, he said, 'But I don't talk like that!' in *exactly* the same way in which Tony had taken him off.

Tony had worked with an impressive roster of directors,

ABOVE AND RIGHT: Danny Wilde and Sir Brett Sinclair doing what they did best on *The Persuaders!*. As you might imagine, Tony and I had a great deal of fun on and off set.

and while he rarely spoke ill of anyone, he did tell me he had a tough time on *Spartacus* with director Stanley Kubrick. The whole cast had endured an agonizingly long shoot, and one day Tony turned to co-star Jean Simmons and asked, 'Who do you have to fuck to get off this picture?'

As part of the package of luring Tony to make a TV series, Lew Grade bought him a house in Chester Square in London's fashionable Belgravia for an astonishing £49,000 – and it was Tony's to keep. A few years later he sold it for £250,000 and thought he'd made a pretty good deal, but a couple of years after that, when he returned to England and looked at buying a similar property, he discovered the asking price was nearer £2 million.

Throughout the fifteen-month shoot, or at least most of it, Tony's wife Leslie was pregnant. She was already 'well endowed', but was now even more ample of bosom. Tony had always been what you'd call a 'boob man', and so he liked Leslie to wear low-cut dresses that exposed as much as possible. One evening I was at his house for a party and, as his wife walked into the room, Tony said to the assembled throng, 'Look at my darling Leslie, doesn't she have the most wonderful tits?'

In between set-ups one day on set Tony said, 'Dear sweet Roger, Burt Lancaster once told me that if you're in your dressing room at the studio with a young lady and your wife should walk in, continue with what you're doing and when you get home deny it, and say, "But they have people who look like me."'

I was never tempted into such a situation, though a year or two later I found myself filming in South Africa, and in one scene my character was to bed a rather attractive young lady in her apartment, demonstrating his Bond-like masculinity no doubt, and in a very thick Afrikaans accent the young actress said to me, 'I really wish there weren't all these people around', referring, of course, to the crew.

'Oh, why?' I asked innocently.

'Because I could show you a really good time!' I thought about Tony's words for a split second, but that thought soon turned to my (then) Italian wife, who was sitting downstairs and who knew my stunt double was off that day!

The Persuaders! was scheduled for a twelve-month shoot but ended up taking fifteen. You see, not only did Tony like to wander off script and improvise on occasions, meaning we found ourselves taking a little longer to shoot a particular sequence, he had a total aversion to overtime.

The British Trade Unions were all powerful at this time, and the ACTT (Association of Cinematograph Television and Allied Technicians) had very strict rules about working hours, with the only exception being you could 'call the quarter' (an extra fifteen minutes) if the red 'shooting' light was on at 5.30 p.m. and you needed to finish a certain scene.

Tony got wise to this, and would never start a scene after 5.15 p.m.!

We also found it particularly difficult to persuade him to come in for looping. This is the process undertaken at the end of all movies to make sure the soundtrack is consistent in each scene or to add music.

'But why do we need to do it?' Tony – a veteran of twenty years in movies – asked.

'Tony, in the last set-up in the gardens there was a close-up of me talking, and then it cut to you but an aeroplane was flying over at that point. So when we edit it together it'll go from no background noise on me, to noise on you, to no noise on me again ... we need to re-record your dialogue,' I explained.

'Audiences are sophisticated,' he replied in all seriousness. 'They understand these things.'

Knowing he didn't want to stay back after 5.30 p.m., when it was usual to loop any such scenes, I suggested we might do it during our lunchtime for half an hour.

'Okay, okay,' he conceded. 'But I want champagne and smoked salmon in the theatre.'

The next day, he arrived at the theatre in Pinewood and a few moments later Johnny Goodman, our Associate Producer, just happened to walk in.

'Tony!' Johnny shouted. 'Smoked salmon and champagne! You've never had it so good!'

'Goddam son of a bitch!' Tony shouted. 'You've just blown your half hour!' and he stormed out.

Tony was what you might call 'very careful' with his money, to the point you might have actually wondered if his trouser pockets were sewn up. One Christmas, we were shooting *The Persuaders!* over the Festive period and he invited my (then) wife and I to join him and Leslie for dinner one night. I'll never forget it: he produced the tiniest roast chicken, which, we discovered, was to serve not only us four, but his two household staff as well. Talk about trying to pick the meat off the bones!

Just then a group of carol singers arrived outside the front door and piped up with 'Once In Royal David's City'. At the end of it, they rang the bell in expectation of receiving a little Christmas offering. Tony started waving his arms and screamed like a banshee, 'Get away, get away or I'll call the cops!'

Leslie, who obviously felt pleased at having picked up a little English, said, 'No, Tony! It's Bobbies, honey, *Bobbies*!'

His meanness was demonstrated further at the end of

filming, when it is customary for the leading actors to be offered some of the items of clothing they had worn in the production. Tony took absolutely everything, and then held a sale for the crew to come over and buy it all off him!

He next called Johnny Goodman to his dressing room.

'Well, Johnny, we've been working together for fifteen months and I'd like to give you something in appreciation of everything you've done for me.'

Johnny, being somewhat surprised at this out-of-character generosity, thanked Tony profusely – and was duly presented with a bottle of the cheapest sherry you could buy from the local supermarket.

'Now, what shall I write on it?' Tony pondered aloud. 'I know ...' and he scribbled 'Best wishes, Tony'.

Johnny has never opened it, and often stares at it ... in disbelief.

But you couldn't help but love Tony, he was a terrific character and a gift as a co-star.

Meanness is not an attractive trait in actors, and I remember a production accountant telling me he had been working with a certain thespian of Scottish origin and had arranged for his *per diem* (agreed daily out-of-pocket expenses) to be dropped into the actor's dressing room each morning.

'Keep hold of it until the end of the week, would you?' the actor said each morning. Then at the end of the week he said, 'I don't need it at present, so keep hold of it until I come and see you.'

A couple of months later, with filming complete, there was a stack of these little brown envelopes in the safe, and together they amounted to a considerable sum. The actor came to collect them with a large briefcase.

The following week bills started arriving from restaurants, theatres, car companies – the actor had charged everything he should have paid with his *per diem* to the production and pocketed the cash!

Whatever his eccentricities, though, Tony ensured that there was never a dull day when we were making *The Persuaders!*. Over our fifteen-month schedule we filmed in every nook and cranny of Pinewood and the adjoining Black Park.

❧

Cubby Broccoli was a regular in the Pinewood dining room and always made a point of introducing me to his guests. He sat at the large round table – the same one that had been reserved for Emeric Pressburger all those years earlier – where he entertained backers, sponsors, royalty and visiting journalists over sumptuous lunches. It was a magical environment in which to impress visitors and inveigle finance. Stars such as Bette Davis, James Caan, Peter Ustinov, Katharine Hepburn, David Niven, Gregory Peck, Stewart Granger, Richard Burton and Elizabeth Taylor could all be spotted at the tables. Liz would be showing off her latest jewel, and they'd talk about who was doing what next and for how much, or what offers they'd refused, or gossip about who was sleeping with whom, all often punctuated by the unmistakable laugh of Sid James and the *Carry On* gang on neighbouring tables.

'How many set-ups did you get in this morning?' Sid would shout across, inducing a sort of friendly rivalry to anyone in earshot (he'd no doubt taken side bets on it). Tony Curtis was once prompted to boast that we'd managed 'five'.

ABOVE: The *Carry On* films were in their early days when this shot was taken in the 1960s, but Barbara Windsor and the gang were always around at Pinewood, and we enjoyed a friendly rivalry in the dining room.

'Oh, we slipped in eight,' Barbara Windsor chuckled back, much to Tony's chagrin.

Meanwhile, the *Carry On* producer Peter Rogers locked the stage doors at lunchtime to prevent any of his artistes or crew claiming overtime.

Kenneth Williams starred in more of the *Carry On* films than any other actor, though he never stopped complaining about what he felt were poor scripts, terrible money and co-stars with whom he didn't get along. However, his moaning and bitching aside, he was without doubt one of the funniest raconteurs you could ever meet. When I started on my first book tour in 2008, I was reminded of the story Kenneth told about attending a store signing in Australia – though actually he stole the story from Monica Dickens, to whom it actually happened, but we won't let that detract from my tale.

'Who's it for?' he asked the lady at the front of the queue.

'Emma Chisset.'

He duly signed and handed her the book.

'What's this?' asked the lady, looking at the inscription.

'Your name!' exclaimed Williams.

'No, I didn't say "*Emma Chisset*", I asked "*Ha much issit?*"'

Aside from his acting work, and borrowing other people's stories, Kenneth also took great pride in another job within the industry, which not a lot of people know about.

When director Kevin Connor and casting director Allan Foenander set out in search of a young leading lady for *Arabian Adventure* in the late 1970s, they scoured the length and breadth of Britain without success, but then someone suggested they go and see a young girl at drama school by the name of Emma Samuelson. They were absolutely bowled over by the young actress and Kevin was in no doubt that he'd found his young lead. However, there was a problem: being still in drama school, Emma was not yet a member of the actors' union Equity and as such wouldn't be allowed to work on a British film. Ironically, the rules at the time stated that she would not be able to get her Equity ticket until she had a certain number of paid acting jobs under her belt. It was quite a ridiculous situation, but the union was all-powerful back then. All was not lost though as, in extraordinary circumstances, Equity might consider waiving the rule provided they could be convinced there was no one else suitable for the part.

Kevin, Allan and producer John Dark convened a meeting at Pinewood for the visiting Equity representative, in the knowledge it was really make or break for young Emma's film career – and the picture. They sat solemnly waiting for the rep to arrive ... and in walked Kenneth Williams, with his trademark nostrils flaring.

The trio argued the case for casting Emma, and a stern and very serious Kenneth asked, 'And there is no member of Equity who could play this role?'

'No, we've cast extensively and Emma really is the only one suitable,' replied Kevin Connor.

'Then, in the circumstances, we shall offer Miss Samuelson membership and permission to be contracted.'

Despite taking his union role very seriously, he couldn't help but then let his guard down over tea and biscuits and revert to his outrageous self, telling everyone about his recent 'bum trouble'.

Incidentally, producer John Dark said that the name 'Emma Samuelson' would be too long to appear on cinema marquees and so shortened it to Samms. And so began the career of a wonderful actress.

The first Bond girl, Eunice Gayson, had a similar discussion with her employers. She was born 'Eunice Sargaison' and when she secured her first West End play, the producer – who paid for signage out in front of the theatre by the letter – said she must shorten her name. Funny how these things happen, isn't it? And as for my old mate Maurice Micklewhite, his agent suggested it wasn't the sort of name that tripped off the tongue easily, so young Maurice looked across from the phone box at Leicester Square where he was calling from and saw *The Caine Mutiny* was playing at the Odeon. Henceforth Michael Caine, film star, was born.

Kenneth Williams, meanwhile, had a habit of flashing his manhood around the Pinewood sets. 'Oh no, Kenny, put it away!' his female co-stars would moan. I think he did it more in an attempt to shock than anything else, although I did hear on one occasion that he complained to producer Peter Rogers that he had 'grazed his penis' on set and was sent off to see the nurse. Twenty minutes later, and with his director and co-stars waiting, there was still no sign of Williams, so Peter marched down to the nurse's office, opened the door and saw him lying on the table naked, sighing gently, while the nurse was massaging his tool with a handful of ointment.

'I'll be there in a few minutes,' replied the star, as Peter almost wet himself with laughter.

On another occasion, at a party thrown by comedy actress Betty Marsden, the hostess said to Williams, 'Now, Kenneth, are you behaving yourself?'

'Is my cock hanging out?' he asked.

'No,' she said, cautiously.

'Well then, I must be!' said Kenny.

Kenneth – unlike me, of course – took great pleasure in talking about his various ailments whenever he was on the chat show circuit, such as the occasion he was in his theatre dressing room, washing his rear end in a pot, when Noël Coward sprang through the door to congratulate him on his performance. Kenneth apologized for his appearance, and said that following his last operation, the doctor had advised that he should bathe rather than use paper after visiting the loo.

'My dear boy,' replied the Master, 'you have no need to explain. I had that very operation and know just how painful piles can be.'

'Piles! Oh nooooooo,' protested Williams, 'I don't have them! I have pipilles.'

Without missing a beat, Coward replied, 'Pipilles, dear boy, is an island in the South Seas.'

❧

I can't write about Pinewood and not mention the biggest film never made there, can I? *Cleopatra* with Elizabeth Taylor in the title role, Richard Burton as Mark Antony and Rex Harrison as Julius Caesar (though that part was actually cast with Peter Finch when production commenced in 1960). So many problems plagued the film, not least the runaway budget which, at the time, made it the most expensive film that had ever come out of the studio. In fact the trouble started when the proposed leading lady, Joan Collins, was rejected by director Rouben Mamoulian in favour of Elizabeth Taylor who demanded – and got – the previously unheard-of fee of $1million for her participation.

Following that huge investment, lavish sets of previously unprecedented dimensions were constructed on the back lot, including the harbour in Alexandria (which held one million gallons of water – that'd take a few days with a bucket, I'll bet) and the Egyptian desert, but the construction coincided with a plasterers' strike and, in desperation, the studio took out advertising on prime-time TV to fill the vacancies. Before even a foot of film had been exposed, the expenditure had exceeded £1 million.

Then there were the 5,000 extras to accommodate with extra trains, buses and shuttles and mobile toilets that were brought in from Epsom racecourse. But the one thing the financiers didn't bank on when they opened their wallets was the British weather. Torrential rain fell and shooting was abandoned. Worse still, Elizabeth Taylor fell dangerously ill and had to undergo an emergency tracheotomy, and Joan Collins was put on standby to replace her. But with the rain still falling incessantly, and Liz Taylor's recuperation likely to be a long one, the decision was made to relocate to a warmer climate, which would help aid their star's recovery, and so everyone shipped out to Rome to remount the production. Well, except for Finchie – he'd had enough. Rouben Mamoulian also left the production at that point and was replaced by Joseph Mankiewicz.

Spotting an opportunity to use some of the leftover sets and costumes, producer Peter Rogers made *Carry On Cleo* and at one point fell foul of 20th Century Fox by emulating their posters. It wasn't the first time that had happened either, as when Peter made *Carry On Spying* the Bond producers raised their concerns about his poster looking similar to *From Russia With Love*.

While we on the Bond films had the luxury of six-month schedules and generous budgets, the *Carry Ons* were made for a few hundred thousand pounds and shot in about five weeks, with only occasional location work outside the studio – usually in Maidenhead. When *Carry On Up the Khyber* was made they used Snowdonia in Wales to double for the Afghan mountains (again no expense lavished) and at the premiere, one of the invited dignitaries sidled up to the producer and said he'd served in the Army and, 'I remember so many of those locations in Afghanistan and India. What marvellous memories.' Peter Rogers didn't have the heart to tell him the truth. But that is the magic of movies.

Donald Sinden told me a great story about working at the studios, a story that typifies the ethos at the studio at that time. Donald was a familiar face at Pinewood as a Rank contract star and later on in the 1970s I worked with him on a film called *That Lucky Touch*. He used to love chatting about all the people he'd worked with and is a brilliant raconteur. Apparently he was in the bar at Pinewood one day, and bumped into the producer Joe Janni, who started telling Donald about a script that involved three months' location work cruising around the Greek islands. On hearing that, Donald said, 'Count me in!' and didn't even wait to read the script.

A few weeks before shooting, Janni called to say that, unfortunately, the budget wouldn't stretch to the Greek islands. It was to be the Channel Islands instead. It still sounded good though. However, a week or so before shooting, Donald went for a costume fitting and the wardrobe man said, 'Shame about the Channel Islands, isn't it?'

Donald didn't know what he meant … until the wardrobe man explained that the budget wouldn't stretch to the Channel Islands … and the location was now Tilbury docks near London! They shot out to sea on one side, turned the ship around and shot the other way, and spent three months in those wretched docks … the magic of the movies indeed!

※

Another great friend in the early years was Kenneth More. Kenny and I met in 1962 when he was filming *We Joined the Navy* at ABPC Elstree and I was filming my first series of *The Saint* on the next stage. We struck up an immediate friendship and saw one another all the time thereafter.

ABOVE: My dear friend Kenny More was best man on my wedding day, 11 April 1969, seen here with his wife Angela Douglas.

Kenny had been a huge star over at Pinewood for Rank, starring in films such as *Genevieve*, *Reach for the Sky* and *Sink the Bismarck!* and in 1960 Rank's managing director, John Davis, agreed to release him to appear in a big-budget film at Shepperton Studios called *The Guns of Navarone*. However, shortly before production commenced, Kenny made the mistake of heckling and swearing at Davis at a BAFTA dinner, and in one fell swoop lost both the role (which went to David Niven) and his contract with Rank.

At the time we met, Kenny was filing for divorce from his wife, Billie, as he'd fallen in love, and wanted to be with, Angela Douglas. I was, meanwhile, in the throes of seeking a divorce from Dot Squires. It's fair to say we both wondered if we'd ever receive a *decree absolute* as the legal wranglings went on for years.

Kenny and I made a pact that we would both be each other's best man when we were finally able to remarry – he was the first, in March 1968, whereas I had to wait a little longer. In fact, I remember one time we were in Mario & Franco's restaurant in Soho and we had a discussion about what colour our respective wives-to-be wedding dresses should be. I suggested grey for my intended ... they say hell hath no fury like a woman scorned, and did I feel hell's full fury that day!

Kenny was a shrewd man when it came to the business as, unlike some actors who think they are invincible, he knew his limitations and also what type of roles suited him. I know Sir Peter Hall suggested that he play Claudius to Albert Finney's Hamlet at the Royal National Theatre, but Kenny declined, saying, 'One part of me would have liked to, but the other part said that there were so many great Shakespearian actors who could have done it better. I stick to the roles I can play better than them.'

Sadly Kenny was forced to retire in 1980, when it was announced that he was suffering from Parkinson's disease. I regret not seeing as much of Kenny as I should have in his final years, but being mainly based in Hollywood and he in London it wasn't terribly easy.

Albert Finney was another of the great British actors of that time. I remember meeting Albie when he and his theatre-producing partner Michael Medwin were in Gstaad, though of course I had known him from his many great films. His breakthrough hit was probably *Saturday Night and Sunday Morning*, which was produced by Harry Saltzman, and afterwards Harry placed Albie under some sort of contract, the terms of which meant that when not employing Albie, Harry still stood to gain from renting him out.

When a call came from legendary producer Sam Spiegel, wanting to see Albie for *Lawrence of Arabia*, which David Lean was to direct, Harry sent him off post-haste to Shepperton. On his return Harry asked how it went.

'He blew smoke in my face,' said Albie.

'What are you talking about?' asked Harry.

'He blew fucking smoke in my face!' said the aggrieved star.

Apparently, Spiegel sat behind his desk at the studio smoking a big cigar throughout the interview and, perhaps not unreasonably, Albie resented it. A few days later, the phone rang and the message came through that Spiegel wanted to shoot some footage of Albie on set the following Monday, so he was obviously odds-on for the role.

'OK, you'll be there at 10 a.m. on Monday,' Harry said.

Nonplussed, Albie looked straight at Harry: 'No! He fucking blew smoke in my face!'

Later that evening Harry called Lew Wasserman, the doyen of agents and dealmakers, in California to tell him the situation.

'Get me Finney on the phone,' Lew barked back at Harry.

Harry had to then telephone around Albie's various girlfriends to find out which one he was shacked up with that week.

'Lew Wasserman wants to speak to you from Palm Springs about *Lawrence of Arabia*,' Harry said, when he finally tracked him down.

Albie dutifully phoned Wasserman back. 'Spiegel blew smoke in my fucking face!'

'It doesn't matter what he did!' Wasserman argued. 'Get your ass down to Shepperton at ten o'clock on Monday morning!'

'But I told you, he blew smoke in my face!'

'Look. Do you know who the hell I am?' asked Wasserman.

'Yes,' said Albie. 'You're my fucking agent – and he *still* blew smoke in my fucking face!'

On another occasion Albie was appearing with Charles Laughton in a production of *The Party* and every time Albie started his big speech, Laughton would very visibly start scratching his nose or arse, and generally making distracting moves. Albie suffered it a few nights and then told Harry Saltzman to 'Tell Mr Laughton I'll kick him into the orchestra pit if he fucking does that again.'

'Oh will he?' chuckled Laughton.

'He WILL!' Harry replied matter-of-factly.

That's what I love about Albie, he is completely independent and speaks his mind without fear of upsetting anyone. Needless to say, he didn't go to Shepperton or get the part of Lawrence, though it never hampered his career. Nowadays he doesn't have an agent, he prefers to negotiate through his lawyer and you won't find him at film premieres or awards ceremonies as he hates all that – he'll turn up, give a great performance and then go home. That's what Albie does. He turned down both a CBE and Knighthood, saying it 'perpetuated snobbery'. (I guess that makes me a terrible snob?)

⁂

Back at the studio, you'd often find lots of actors and directors would zip away after a thirty-minute lunch to view rushes, which was the previous day's film back from the labs. It wouldn't be out of the ordinary to see a few extras dressed as centurions, or large chickens, cutting through the restaurant to the bar. Nobody flinched. It was, after all, a place of work.

Lunchtimes at the studio saw other regulars too, one being Christopher Reeve who'd walk in for his meal in full Superman costume. He was so polite and would always stop at the tables he passed to say hello to fellow diners. Many a waitress swooned after him.

The bar was quite a 'club' too. Often you'd find Peter Finch holding court at lunchtimes and evenings with tales of the outback and working in Hollywood. He and Diane Cilento once naughtily inserted a cigarette into the mouth of a rather expensive *Laughing Cavalier*-type painting on the wall, much to the annoyance of Peter Rogers, who'd just paid to have it restored. Finchie was very much the practical joker of Pinewood, hiding in cupboards to surprise passers-by, removing gargoyles from the entrance and taking them home, and jackarooing around the bar with Diane at lunchtime, rounding up the crew.

He was a wonderful character. British born, though raised in Australia, he probably received greatest acclaim for his last film, *Network* – for which he posthumously received the Academy Award. I believe the only other person to win an Oscar after his death was another Australian, Heath Ledger – as my friend Michael Caine might say, not a lot of people know that.

Finchie very nearly didn't make it to his career in Hollywood, or Pinewood for that matter, as, when aged just nineteen, he almost died when he was in Melbourne for a play called *So This is Hollywood*. The cast all went out for a picnic one day and afterwards he and co-star Robert Capron took off for a walk to explore the Pound Bend Tunnel on the Yarra River at Warrandyte, Victoria. Finchie told me they saw a fox terrier puppy fall into the river and Capron dived in and tried to save it. Tragically the current proved too strong and despite Finchie's best efforts to save him, Capron drowned. Ironically, the dog survived and Finchie was later awarded a certificate of merit by the Humane Society, though I don't think he ever got over losing his friend; it weighed on his mind for the rest of his life.

In his obituary notices Finchie was invariably described as a 'hell-raiser' and to a great extent his drinking, womanizing and larger-than-life antics overshadowed his prolific acting career. In a poignant interview shortly before his untimely death in 1977, aged just sixty, he said:

'I'd like to have been more adventurous in my career. But it's a fascinating and not ignoble profession. No one lives more lives than the actor. Movie-making is like geometry and I hated maths. But this kind of jigsaw I relish. When I played Lord Nelson I worked the poop deck in his uniform. I got extraordinary shivers. Sometimes I felt like I was staring at my own coffin. I touched that character. There lies the madness. You can't fake it.'

❧

My next visit to Pinewood after *The Persuaders!* was in 1973 as Jimmy Bond. Cubby Broccoli had had any number of offers to take the series overseas, but no, he said, 'Pinewood is my home.' It wasn't just sentimentality, it was good business sense as the crews always delivered the very best and Cubby loved the environment.

Along with the good fortune and success, I've also seen Pinewood at its lowest ebb. When we went in to shoot *Octopussy* there was nothing, and I mean nothing, else in the studio – no other films were being made. The whole industry

ABOVE: In between Bond films I earned a few bob playing Father
Christmas. Listening to the little ones and their expectations
from Santa was a treat I couldn't miss.

was in the doldrums. Word had it that had we not returned it would have closed down. Shepperton shared a similar fate, with changes of ownership and asset-strippers bringing the studio to near collapse and closure. Soon afterwards, Pinewood was forced to go 'four-walled' – becoming a rental facility, rather than a fully crewed studio.

The studio quickly diversified into commercials and more TV work. The plan paid off and meant that scores of big-budget blockbuster movies all had a home in the British countryside, though at the turn of the century its future seemed unsure when in 2000 the Rank Organisation announced plans to pull out of all its film interests, including Pinewood; but a new hero was at hand to continue the Pinewood story. Enter Michael Grade.

I knew Michael of old, his uncle was Lew Grade of the Incorporated Television Company (ITC), and Michael was every bit as passionate about film and TV as Lew was, but he's also a very astute businessman. He spotted the potential and value of Pinewood and pulled together a financial consortium to buy the famous studio. He then made an offer to Ridley and Tony Scott, the owners of Shepperton, to merge the two studios.

The place is now much bigger than it was in 1947, with twenty stages as opposed to just five, and more on-site companies and services than you can shake a stick at, but the atmosphere remains the same. It is, I have decided, pure magic.

CHAPTER 3

Stage-struck

'YOU CAN'T BE A SERIOUS ACTOR UNTIL YOU'VE TROD THE boards first!' was the adage of the old Shakespearian actors who toured until they dropped. They were quite inspiring to a young, hungry actor, though. While I spent much of the free time of my youth at the Odeon cinema in Streatham, south London, I also enjoyed visiting music halls and what you'd now call fringe theatres. One actor I seemed to follow around was a deliciously macabre chap named Tod Slaughter.

He was unintentionally hysterical and so over the top, playing maniacal villains with rolling eyes, a mad cackling laugh and over-exaggerated mannerisms. He was typecast to the point of being known as 'Mister Murder' and usually played in Victorian melodramas like *Sweeney Todd*, *Burke and Hare* and *Jack the Ripper*. In the latter, at the end of the play he was 'killed' on stage and I remember one night when the curtains came down his feet were left sticking out beneath the curtain. His size tens were slowly withdrawn, only for him to reappear in front of the tabs seconds later

LEFT: Tod Slaughter – looks a friendly chap, doesn't he?

for his obligatory, and highly theatrical, curtain speech:

'Ladies and gentlemen, our story has been taken from the annals of Scotland Yard and is true in every aspect except the Ripper was never caught. But you saw him killed before your very eyes tonight and can now leave this theatre safe in the knowledge that you ladies don't have to wonder, "Is he there? Is he there?" when you walk into the darkness.'

These monologues were often better than the play and Slaughter was certainly the last of the great barnstormers, ceaselessly touring the provinces in his hoary old melodramas right up until the day he died.

Talking of ladies leaving the theatre safely, my former wife, Dorothy Squires – who was not a particularly tall person out of heels, and so liked to wear quite high ones – exited the stage door at the Brixton Empress one night when some lout on a bicycle came up behind her and 'goosed' her, leaving his thumb in her rear end so all she could do was totter along, screaming for help as he pushed her along. Ever after, she always looked left and right for cyclists.

Another film star of my youth who I also saw on stage was Lancastrian comic and music hall entertainer Frank Randle, who actually only made ten movies and usually without his false teeth in. He often fell foul of the censors, particularly in Blackpool where they banned him from performing some of his material on stage, and it's fair to

RIGHT: With my wife, Dorothy Squires. Dot made her name on radio shows such as *Variety Bandbox*, and then went on to success in the US.

say Randle did not take kindly to criticism or hecklers and would throw his dentures at them as a mark of protest. His many run-ins with the police led to a significant charge sheet being lodged with the Lancashire Constabulary!

He once performed at my local, the Hackney Empire, and when the resident comic came on, Frank appeared on stage and started talking over him, stepping on all his punch-lines. Someone called from the audience, 'Why don't you shut up and let the other comic have a word?'

'You bastards!' shouted Randle. 'You fucking ungrateful bastards!' Next thing I knew, the iron safety curtain came down and he was dragged off stage.

Randle had his caravan parked around the back of the theatre, and immediately let the tyres down so the management couldn't evict him from the premises. He then stood in its doorway, posing for the press with his shirt undone to the waist, showing off his torso.

A friend of mine was part of Randle's travelling theatre company and for the only time in the history of show business the pantomime they were performing, in Birmingham, went on strike.

'Ungrateful bastards!' Randall shouted at the cast. 'Who employs you?'

'You do, Frank, but you haven't paid us,' they reasoned.

'Well, I fucking employ you! What more do you want?'

The dressing rooms were all interconnected and the company discovered that by placing a glass on the radiator pipes they could listen in to Frank talking in the dressing room next door. One day they heard him talking to a police inspector. 'Aye, that second lead of mine, he's an iron hoof I tell you – he's taking it up the bum. And that tall blond London chap, he's been shoplifting and bragging about it.'

They realized that Frank was saying the most terrible things about the actors in order to get them arrested, so that he could get out of paying them.

❦

Jimmy Wheeler was another music hall comedian I followed and got to know. He was a huge man who would come on stage with a violin, and his catchphrase was 'Aye, aye, that's ya lot!'

A friend of mine was working with him in Australia and apparently one day Jimmy got into a taxi and banged the door hard shut. When they reached their destination the driver said, 'I'll thank you not to bang the door.'

Without missing a beat, Jimmy replied, 'The only doors I want to bang is Diana fucking Dors!'

He was once on the same variety bill as Dorothy Squires in Great Yarmouth. Dot was to close the show, while Wheeler was set to go on last in the first half. However, as the interval began drawing nearer, they couldn't find Wheeler. Dot, who was in the dressing room dressed in only her bra and knickers, suddenly heard her entrance music playing.

'Quick, Dot! We need you on!' came the call.

Dot threw on her dress, dashed out on stage and started singing, while the manager of the ABC was dispatched to the local pubs to look for Wheeler. Eventually they found him, half cut, propping up a bar:

'Jimmy! You're on!' snapped the manager.

'How am I fucking doing then?' he replied ... and no apology was forthcoming.

On another occasion I remember him chuntering on

about young comedians, and his wife, who had finally got fed up of dear Jimmy, said, 'Why don't you give it a rest, Jimmy? You're only jealous!'

'And why don't you go and lie down for four-and-a-half fucking years?' quipped the great man.

༺❦༻

Another theatrical great who used to like to bend his elbow at a bar was Wilfrid Lawson. He was serving as a Special Constable at Bow Street Police Station during the war – where my dad was also stationed. Part of their daily routine was to go on point duty, controlling the traffic long before traffic lights came into being.

One afternoon, Dad told me that he had to go out and help retrieve Special Constable Lawson from The Strand where, far from directing traffic, he was crawling across the roads on his hands and knees – in full uniform. It was not quite the image the Metropolitan Police wanted to portray.

On another occasion, Lawson was rehearsing a play on stage with Nicol Williamson, but failed to report back after lunch. Williamson went into a violent tirade on stage about what a drunk Lawson was, how unreliable he was and so on. When he paused for breath, Lawson's inimitable voice chirped up from the back of the theatre: 'I thought that speech had been cut!'

I often hear ageing actors today bemoaning the lack of good repertory theatre as a training ground for up-and-coming thespians. I must admit I enjoyed my time in the suburbs, as a young aspiring actor, as not only did the fast-changing programme instil a terrific ability to learn on your feet, it also brought with it a sense of stage discipline, invaluable performing experience and the chance to tackle a fascinating variety of plays. Money was never very generous though and our staple diet often revolved around baked beans on toast and fry-ups.

Sir Donald Wolfit has often been described as the last of the great actor-managers. With his repertory group of players he would travel the provinces bringing the great stories to the masses – well, maybe not quite *masses* but a grateful few at least. Wolfit was an exuberant, larger-than-life personality who was perhaps most famously the inspiration for the character of 'Sir' in the film *The Dresser*, as played by Albert Finney. I'm told by those who knew Wolfit that he was a temperamental and difficult man to deal with and was, like Frank Randle, enraged by any form of criticism. He was also tyrannical with the companies he led. One young actor was put in his place quite firmly when he asked what the next production would be and what his part in it might be: 'I'll ask you if I think you can play some speaking roles by then,' snapped Wolfit.

Wolfit was undoubtedly a fine actor, but one with indifferent feelings about film work – despite making thirty appearances on screen – considering film a 'poor relation' to theatre, though his talent and ambition in theatre was undoubtedly handicapped by the more modest venues he ended up appearing in. The great – if eccentric – English actress Hermione Gingold summed it up best by saying, 'Olivier is a tour-de-force, and Wolfit is forced to tour.'

At the end of each show Wolfit would perform a curtain call speech, much like Tod Slaughter did. One week, he came out front of the tabs and in his 'chewing the scenery' theatrical drawl said: 'Next week, ladies and gentlemen, we shall be bringing you *Macbeth*. I will be playing the title role and my wife ...'

'Your wife is a whore!' came a shout from the gallery.

'Nevertheless,' continued Wolfit, unfazed, 'she will be playing Lady Macbeth ...'

There were many stories and rumours about Wolfit, including him haranguing the people at a cinema queue to leave it and attend the theatre – in another part of town – where his company was playing. Some even suggested that, to earn a few bob on the side, he sold insurance on easy payment terms to actors. I'd like to believe that one!

It's not quite another Wolfit story, but one I'd like to think was from an actor-manager of his ilk (if only of lesser standing) for whom a young Welsh actor named Brian Ellis auditioned. When he offered Brian a role in the company he cautioned him that the pay wasn't very good, but, in a negotiating ploy to seal the deal, he proudly added, 'There is an edible pudding in act two every night.'

On his deathbed, so legend has it, Wolfit was still keen to offer words of wisdom to members of his rep company. One of his young actors asked, 'Sir Donald, after a life so filled with success and fame, dying must be hard ...'

'Dying is easy ... Comedy is hard,' replied the great man.

For some unknown reason, though I think it might well have been jealousy, Wolfit hated Sir John Gielgud and referred to him as 'the Enemy'. It obviously niggled at Gielgud, as when he was invited to speak at Wolfit's memorial programme, produced by the BBC, he responded, 'I couldn't. You see we always regarded him as something of a joke.'

I made a film with Gielgud called *Gold*, though as is typical in this business we never actually met on set as neither of us appeared in a scene together. Gielgud had something of a reputation for putting his foot quite firmly in his mouth, and never really thought about what he was saying until after he'd actually said it. For example, when James Villiers (who played Bill Tanner in *For Your Eyes Only*) assumed Laurence Olivier's role as Victor in *Private Lives*, Olivier later asked Gielgud what his performance was like.

'Oh, Larry, I've never seen the part of Victor so perfectly realized. Oh, sorry, I didn't mean that!'

A great friend (and employer) of Gielgud's was theatre manager and producer Binkie Beaumont, who co-founded the highly successful theatrical production company H.M. Tennent and had control of half the theatres in London's West End. Binkie was a larger-than-life character. Hugely powerful in the London theatre world, he had a very wide and impressive social circle. While I, as a lowly understudy for the firm, was never invited to mix in such company, I did hear a very amusing story about Binkie and Gielgud.

'John is coming over,' Binkie warned his weekend guests at his country home. 'And he is bringing a rather unsuitable young man with him, so be nice.'

Gielgud duly arrived with a young James Dean-type in tow, who, he said, 'wanted to be an actor' and, leaving him with Binkie in the hall, Gielgud went straight through to the kitchen. After a moment or two of awkward silence, Binkie asked, 'Would you like me to show you around, Hector?'

The boy smiled sheepishly, and nodded.

Five or six minutes later, Binkie returned to the kitchen, furious with Gielgud.

'Johnny! That boy is impossible! I took him to the garden and said, "This is the croquet lawn, Hector" and he just grunted. I took him around to the pool, and asked, "Do you swim, Hector?" and he just stood there, staring blankly at me and then stammered over a few incoherent words. And you say he wants to be an actor? He can't even speak the Queen's English!'

'For God's sake, Binkie,' said Gielgud. 'His name is Sebastian! Hector is what I call his cock!'

Gielgud's continuing gaffs really were the stuff of legend, and I remember as he visited the ailing Laurence Olivier towards the end of his life, he reportedly exclaimed, 'Larry! You're dead! I mean ... you're dying! I mean ... my poor darling Larry, you don't look at all well!'

He once upset Richard Burton too, after going to see him backstage following a production of *Hamlet*, 'We'll have dinner when you're better ... I mean when you're ready.'

Despite delivering many fine performances in 'classical' parts on stage and screen, it was for his role as the butler in the film *Arthur* that he was given an Academy Award. He very nearly didn't accept the role, however. 'I turned it down a couple of times ... I thought the script was rather smutty, rather common. They just wanted a posh-looking Englishman saying rather racy things. Every time I said "no" the price went up and finally, when I accepted, they said "how clever of you", which wasn't the case at all.'

Gielgud continued working well into his nineties, though at his own pace and mindful of his advancing years. To keep the insurance companies happy, producers usually scheduled his scenes all fairly tightly together. I remember him saying, 'In my last big parts, I kept thinking, "Suppose

I die in the middle? What is it going to cost everyone?"'

When he was asked to join MPs Glenda Jackson and Gyles Brandreth at the House of Commons for his ninetieth birthday celebrations, he replied, 'Yes, I would be delighted to join them. You see, all my real friends are dead.'

Though perhaps some words of his I should heed, 'When you're my age, you never risk being ill, because everyone then says, "Oh, he's done for."'

⁂

Ah! the roar of the greasepaint and the smell of the crowds! Danny La Rue was unquestionably the most famous Dame – or if you'd prefer, drag act – in all Theatreland. In fact, he was one of Britain's highest-earning entertainers of the 1960s.

In the days of my exposure to the variety world, a married couple who were close friends of Dorothy Squires produced and toured a couple of drag shows and Dot used to sell her old ball gowns to members of the troupe – one of whom was Danny.

Jack, who was the husband in the husband-and-wife-producing team, said to me one day, 'You'd better believe in fairies.'

'Why?' I asked.

'They're real!' Jack exclaimed. 'One night I fired one of my leading ladies, and the next night, when I came out of the stage door, he pointed his unfurled umbrella at me and said, "The witch's curse on you, Jack Lewis!"'

Jack said that at the time he laughed it off and returned to his digs, only to open the newspaper the next morning to see headlines containing allegations about Lord Montagu and boy scouts. That incident, for which Baron Montagu of Beaulieu was jailed for twelve months, killed drag shows for months afterwards. You see, audiences – probably not helped by the press stories – incorrectly associated transvestites and homosexuals with 'doing things with boys'. Jack Lewis lost huge business – and never doubted the curse again.

Danny, meanwhile, with his dazzling coiffures, extravagant costumes, immaculate make-up, false eyelashes and high heels, went on to open a club in London's Hanover Square, where he performed his wonderful impressions of Elizabeth Taylor, Zsa Zsa Gabor, Judy Garland, Marlene Dietrich and many others. He also gave a break to a great many singers and comedians who were desperate for a leg up in show business.

The club became extremely popular for its satirical revues long before *That Was The Week That Was,* and attracted celebrities and royalty – as well as coach parties from all over the country – in huge numbers.

Danny made no bones about 'dressing up in a frock' being just a job, not a lifestyle choice. He enjoyed his job greatly but when off stage, liked his privacy. When Princess Margaret knocked on his dressing-room door after a show one night, a stark naked Danny threw it open and shouted, 'Piss off!'

'I was mortified,' he said. 'I thought she was Peter Sellers messing about!'

꿈꿈

Liberace was another tremendous showman. I met Liberace, or Lee as he liked to be called by his friends, in Hollywood in the very late 1950s – though I can't quite recall how

ABOVE: With Tommy Steele, Dot and Liberace at a party in LA. The hair is real — well, mine, at least.

I came to be invited to the party at his house. But you know me — anything for a free meal. To say the decor was kitsch would be the understatement of all understatements. I remember the ceilings being painted with frescos in the style of Rome's Sistine Chapel and there being ornate marble pillars, diamond-encrusted chandeliers, countless pianos, and many huge paintings and photos of Liberace decorating the house. Everything was done to excess, but that's how Lee liked it.

Lee loved being around actors and he told me he'd always wanted to be a movie star. He did make a couple of films and I think even popped up as a villain in the *Batman* TV series at one point, but it never quite worked out for him in that direction – though he did have his own hugely popular TV shows and guest-starred in many other variety and chat-style programmes.

I found him to be extremely polite, fascinating to talk with and very well read, and while I knew he was an accomplished pianist, it was only when I saw him perform in Vegas that I realized his genius was in taking popular well-known tunes, adding a huge dollop of bling and serving it up with masses of charm. There are many talented pianists and musicians in the world, but there are few who have been able to match his showmanship.

It was relatively well known in Hollywood that Lee was gay, though the image he painted for his fans was of a man who hadn't yet met the right woman. I still remember the huge controversy in the UK when fifty years ago Lee sued the *Daily Mirror* newspaper columnist William Connor (who wrote under the byline Cassandra) for implying that he was homosexual. Cassandra wrote that Liberace was:

'... The summit of sex – the pinnacle of masculine, feminine, and neuter. Everything that he, she, and it can ever want ... a deadly, winking, sniggering, snuggling, chromium-plated, scent-impregnated, luminous, quivering, giggling, fruit-flavoured, mincing, ice-covered heap of mother-love.'

It was the suggestion of him being a mincing mother's boy that led to a six-day hearing, during which Lee categorically denied being homosexual. The jury found for him and awarded a then-record £8,000 in damages (which I'm told would equate to about £500,000 in today's money).

His legion of female fans never doubted his heterosexuality, even when his chauffeur and companion Scott Thorson sued him for palimony in 1982.

When Lee died in 1987, his publicists, agent and doctor gave the cause of death as being heart failure, and everyone believed them. Only later, when an autopsy was called for after the coroner expressed his doubts about the death certificate, was it finally acknowledged he had actually died from an AIDs-related illness. Even in death, Liberace was keen that his image should not be tarnished.

⚜

Invariably, comedians are asked to 'tell us a joke' and magicians to 'show us a trick' and more often than not I'm asked to 'tell us about your practical jokes on set'. Of course, as there were so many over so many years, it's impossible to think of one specifically, and it's not something you necessarily plan or think about beforehand – it's usually a spontaneous reaction to a certain moment in time. The times I've squirted crews with hosepipes, dropped my trousers in a tense dramatic scene, started giggling to put a co-star off, or re-written dialogue, are all well documented elsewhere. But I much prefer talking about things that go wrong, as they're always far more memorable – so long as I'm not always the butt of the cock-up, that is.

The law of averages suggests that when you're in a long-running play, or on a lengthy film shoot, then, despite your best efforts, something, somewhere will mess up. In a film, of course, we have the luxury of 'take two' and a clever editor, but it's not quite the same in theatre.

As a young aspiring actor, I went to see John Gielgud in *Hamlet* at the Haymarket Theatre in London and, as the curtain went up, we discovered the stagehands were still putting the planks in place around the graves, the first gravedigger was

ABOVE: I have rather a name as a practical joker … but thankfully as someone who can take a joke as well, as seen here when I was presented with a rubber octopus during a dining scene in *Octopussy*.

shuffling on to take his place and the stage manager was walking across the back of the set, looking up at the lights. I laughed – but I was probably the only one who did.

When I was in repertory theatre at The Intimate in Palmers Green, I once pushed hard on what I thought was a sticky door only to realize it was in fact a pull-door, and took down the entire set. On another occasion I was in a play called *While Parents Sleep* by Anthony Kimmins (the West End production of which starred Jack Hawkins) and in one scene I'm in a drawing room, having a bit of a fumble with a girl, when suddenly the lights come on and we both leap up to stand behind the settee as Lady Cattering enters. She, in turn, had some dialogue about forgiveness and I then had to bow my head down to her.

In rehearsal I said, 'Wouldn't it be funny if I bowed and banged my head on the settee?' The ensuing silence gave me my answer – no, it would not be!

Come the first night, I bowed down, and quite inadvertently hit my head on the said settee, ending up on my knees, having almost passed out. The audience thought it was hilarious, of course.

Actors have all encountered stubborn doors, sets that wobble and stage revolves that just won't revolve, but there are also the technical bloopers such as phones not ringing on cue, gunshots sounding seconds after the actor has already fallen to the floor and doorbells that never ring, leaving the poor terrified soul awaiting his or her cue no choice but to ad lib. 'Oh! Is that Aunt Agatha at the door? I'm sure I heard her car pull up just now.'

And what about the props that don't behave as they ought to? Such as the time in a provincial tour of *The Importance of Being Earnest* when one character was supposed to pour tea for another, but the handle dropped off the teapot. Or maybe a trap door opens when it shouldn't, as happened in the Broadway production of *Fiddler on the Roof*, in which Nancy Opel broke her elbow.

Depending on the actor, they may prefer to ignore any mishap and continue, or perhaps admit something has gone wrong and let the audiences in on the gag, which can often add to the audience's pleasure as they feel they've then been part of something that doesn't ordinarily occur.

For example, in her 2013 record-breaking run of *The Audience* at the Gielgud Theatre in London's glittering West End, Dame Helen Mirren made more headlines for her performance offstage – namely outside the stage door. Some friends of mine were in the audience on the fateful day. With the first half of the production beleaguered by lighting problems, the interval couldn't come quick enough for the cast. When the interval curtain went down, Dame Helen took the opportunity to apologize to the audience for the technical glitches, which, she told them, were being ironed out, but she also added that she had been incredibly mindful of the noise outside too, which no doubt spoiled the first act for patrons.

She went on to explain that the drumming parade, moving through Soho to promote a gay music festival, had decided to stop outside the stage door for a full eight minutes. While supporting the cause, she didn't feel it fair that they made so much noise during a performance and added, 'I told the band to "shut the f*** up" as people had paid "a lot of f***ing money to watch the show" and that they were "f***ing ruining it".'

One onlooker was later heard to say, 'It was strange to see this little woman in tiara and pearls shouting like that.

It's not the behaviour you'd expect from the Queen.'

Dame Helen received a round of applause, and went on to offer the drumming band free tickets to see the show.

Michael Simkins was starring in a touring production of *Dial M for Murder* and with the murderer revealed in the final scene the curtain was supposed to drop – end of play. However, on one particular evening the stagehand pulled the wrong lever and instead of dropping the tabs, activated the sprinkler system. Thinking on his feet, Michael's co-star, who had just left the stage, popped his head back through to help save the scene and said, 'And you ought to get that leaky roof fixed too!'

Then, of course, there was *Charlie and the Chocolate Factory* at the Theatre Royal Drury Lane in June 2013, and a night the great glass elevator stopped working, leaving Douglas Hodge's Willy Wonka and the child actor playing Charlie stranded above the audience. Within ten minutes they were rescued and the performance continued, with an apology to all from the manager. Mind you, that wasn't quite as serious as in a Californian production of *Aladdin* I read about, in which a magical flying carpet tipped off the actors and left them hanging by their safety harnesses.

Wardrobe malfunctions also play their part, as in the case of Maureen Lipman in *Candida* in which she had opened the play and her skirt fell off, leaving her standing in only a slip while her co-star leapt to her defence, continuing to deliver their dialogue all the while.

It's no wonder that actors corpse with laughter, and when one is set off you can guarantee the rest will follow – all trying extremely hard to keep straight faces.

Perhaps the ultimate stage cock-up was at the Wood Green Empire in 1918 when Chinese magician Chung Ling Soo (or William Ellsworth Robinson, to give him his birth name) was performing his popular bullet-catching trick. A gunpowder flash, used in a second chamber of his revolver, which produced the illusion of the gun being fired, actually ignited the bullet in the main chamber, causing the magician to be shot in the chest. Having never before spoken English on stage while adopting his Chinese persona, Chung Ling Soo was heard to say, 'Something has happened. Lower the curtain.' ... I'm afraid it was curtains for him and no *encore* for the audience.

We actors aren't infallible. Alas, we are only human, as I'm reminded when I read through the obituary columns. It's really quite worrying to see names I know in there, especially of people who are younger than me. Occasionally an actor, who, let's face it, spends much of the working day on stage or set, is reported as having croaked it during a performance and the writer will add, as though hugely consoling, 'he'd have liked to know he died on stage doing what he loved best'. Erm, that's not really very comforting, I assure you!

No one made a career out of things going wrong quite like Tommy Cooper – it was his whole act – though, of course, to be such a bad magician meant he was actually remarkably good at magic. But when he collapsed on stage, live on British TV, the audience laughed hysterically, thinking it was all part of the show.

Similarly, when Eric Morecambe suffered a heart attack after a show in Yorkshire in the late 1960s it wasn't perhaps treated as seriously as it would have been if he hadn't been a comedian. Having returned to his hotel he suffered terrible pains in his upper arm and, recognizing the danger signs, decided to drive himself to hospital, but as the pain spread to his chest, he became unable to continue the journey. Thankfully he was rescued by a passer-by who took him to hospital where, with Eric lying on a trolley waiting to go into the operating theatre, a nurse appeared with a pen and piece of paper and said, 'Before you go, would you mind giving me your autograph?'

Thankfully, Eric didn't 'go' anywhere that night, and dined out on the story for years afterwards. Sadly, he died after appearing in a Q&A session at a theatre in Tewkesbury, collapsing in the wings after a standing ovation.

Sid James also passed away at a theatre, but he did it on stage at the Sunderland Empire in front of a packed auditorium. Theatre manager Roy Todds phoned *The Mating Game*'s producer, Bill Robertson, to tell him the shocking news, 'Sid James has just died in Sunderland!'

'Don't worry,' replied Bill. 'Everybody dies in Sunderland.'

CHAPTER 4

On-set Tales

I'VE BEEN FORTUNATE TO WORK WITH SOME WONDERFUL actors – and I've also heard some wonderful stories about some actors I've not worked with!

Although I had a smattering of colloquial Italian, I never really understood the call sheets on my 1962 epic *The Rape of the Sabines*. The film was also known as *Romulus and the Sabines*, and I had the pleasure of playing the role of our hero, Romulus. Though based at studios in Rome, we went off on various random locations too, and I got into the routine of just turning up at the studio and being ready to go wherever we were needed. One day we headed north, at least I think it was north: you could never really hear anything the driver was saying because of incessant chatter coming from the crew on board the bus.

At the first location stop I had a scene with the lovely Italian actress Scilla Gabel, before we then moved up high

LEFT: Frank Sinatra, Montgomery Clift, Deborah Kerr and Burt Lancaster, leaving for location filming of *From Here to Eternity* in the early 1950s. Burt Lancaster was a wonderful actor but boy did he have a terrible temper at times!

into a mountain range, where I remember there was a beautiful limpid blue pool, fed by a little stream, which in turn flowed down from the top of the mountain. It was very picturesque, and easy to see why the location manager had suggested it.

All the extras – women who had been kidnapped by the Romans, under my character's command – began bathing quite merrily and swimming around the pool. One in particular, a former Miss Austria, created quite a bit of interest among the crew in her wet top – they gazed at her with what can best be described as primitive lust and longing. A couple of minutes later the assistant director

BELOW: *The Rape of the Sabines* was memorable, but perhaps for all the wrong reasons … Romulus is seen here with screen parents Rosanna Schiaffino as Venus and Jean Marais as Mars.

shouted, 'OK! Now we'll shoot the South American version.'

I didn't remember ever reading anything about filming other versions of scenes in my contract, so asked what was happening.

'Don't worry,' I was told. 'You're not in it. Just go and take a seat.'

So, that's what I did.

Suddenly all the ladies started taking off their tops – thus creating even greater interest among the crew, so much so that some of them actually stopped chatting. But what we didn't know was that, high up in the mountain, there was some sort of reservoir, from which, when a switch was thrown, a mini, ice-cold, Niagara rushed down into our limpid pool, making it a raging torrent. The women started screaming and the gallant crew gathered by the pool side, to help pull them out – with the exception of Miss Austria, whose bust was acting as a rather splendid buoyancy aid, carrying her fast across to the far side of the pool.

With them all being good Catholics, I can't quite imagine which South American country would have ordered the slightly more risqué version of our film but I do know that it wasn't only this production that had 'alternative' scenes filmed. My (later) producing partner Bob Baker made a number of movies in the UK long before he brought *The Saint* to TV screens. One of them, *Jack the Ripper*, was shot at Shepperton Studios on a 'closed set' – and with good reason. The scene involved a theatre's backstage dressing room, and all the young actresses were in there busy putting on their make-up, dressed only in petticoats and bras, while preparing for curtain up. That was considered lurid enough for the UK censors of the 1950s, but when the scene was in

ABOVE: Angie Dickinson was wonderful to work with on *The Sins of Rachel Cade*. The film was set in the sweat and heat of the Belgian Congo ... but filmed entirely on the sweaty Warner back lot, with footage from *The Nun's Story* for the location scenes.

the bag the assistant director, matter-of-factly, called, 'OK, cut! Clothes off for the continental version now!'

Their petticoats and bras were swiftly dispensed with and the same scene was shot again – only with more in it, if you follow me.

One of these such scenes was filmed on a Friday afternoon very near to the 4 p.m. wrap time, but all the electricians and stage hands willingly offered to stay on to help oversee the 'continental' version being filmed – and no overtime was requested!

One of the more pleasurable bonuses of being an actor is not only to meet but to work with other actors whom you have admired in the past, and Ray Milland was one of those. Ray was born Reginald Alfred John Truscott-Jones, but took his stage name from a riverside street called Milland Road in Neath, South Wales, where he once lived.

I worked with Ray on *Gold* in 1974 and he, rather like Niven, was a great teller of amusing tales, one being of when he was working on a film on location in Africa and a male member of the cast turned up two weeks ahead of schedule. The director asked said actor why he had come so early and he told a story of being at a dinner party in Beverly Hills a couple of nights earlier, and seated next to a rather attractive young lady from the East Coast who was complaining of jetlag, having arrived from New York the day before. The actor suggested that he had some sleeping suppositories that worked wonders for him, and that he would be happy to let her have a couple. As she was staying at the Beverly Hills Hotel he said he'd happily give her a lift back, and stop off at his place on the way to pick up the pills.

Upon arriving home, he thought it would be only polite to ask her in for a drink, and as the night was still young she obviously thought it was a good idea as well and a few minutes later they were drinking Jack Daniels in his living room. He popped into his bedroom for the suppositories.

'They will take about half an hour to take effect,' he explained.

'Good,' she said. 'Maybe you would put one of them in for me now, and then be so kind as to drop me at the hotel?'

The lights in his living room were rather low, so he asked her to bend over close to a lamp, enabling him to see what he was doing. She raised her skirt and bent down and as she lowered her underwear he took up a position behind. Just as he was about to put the suppository in the required position, the door opened and in walked his wife. She was supposed to be in Palm Springs. With there being no believable explanation about him performing an act of kindness to a jetlagged lady, he decided to leave for the location early. Very early.

'Who was the actor?' I asked Ray.

'Can't you guess?' he smiled.

BELOW: With Ray Milland in *Gold* in 1974. This one was filmed in South Africa, but only after a technicians' dispute was averted. We almost had to film it in Wales!

I performed an act of kindness for Ray myself – though not with a suppository, I hasten to add. Ray was suffering with a prostate problem during our filming together and found it very difficult to urinate. He suffered particularly great pain during a late-night shoot and I sympathized greatly because over the years I had suffered terribly with renal colic which, for the uninitiated, is way up at the top of the hit parade for being the most painful experience a man can undergo – they do say that having a child can 'maybe' be as painful. As a precaution against having an attack while away filming, my urologist had prescribed powerful painkillers for me to carry and I duly offered one to Ray. I'm sure that medics would recoil in horror at the thought of one hypochondriac actor giving prescription drugs to another, but needs must at times, and he found almost immediate relief and was able to finish the night's filming.

Towards the end of his career Ray took on a number of, well, less-than-brilliant roles. When asked in an interview why he had appeared in so many bad films, he smiled and said, 'For the money, old chap, for the money!'

❧

In 1976 I made another foray into Italian cinema, signing up for a film called *The Street People* ... no, *The Executioners* ... no, *Opium Road* ... ah yes, *The Sicilian Cross*. It kept changing title but on paper it sounded quite promising, with a script by, among others, Ernest Tidyman, who'd written *The French Connection*. At that time I had a holiday home in Italy, and an Italian wife, so the idea of working there (and in San Francisco too) was rather appealing.

It was essentially the tale of how a Mafia boss is wrongly suspected of smuggling a heroin shipment into San Francisco from Sicily, inside a cross donated to a church there, and so dispatches his nephew, a hotshot lawyer (that's me, being typecast again!), to identify the real culprit. Along the way, I enlist the aid of my best friend, Grand Prix driver Stacy Keach, who has a penchant for destroying anything in his way. Well, that's the essence of the story, but the rest of it – and the finished film – I don't really understand … and neither did cinema audiences to be honest.

In an attempt to explain away my casting, lines such as: 'The smartest thing I ever did was to get you out of Sicily and into that English law school,' and 'Being half-English, half-Sicilian was a good deal for both of us', were written in.

Stacy was a delight to work with, and huge fun, but apart from him and me, all the cast and crew were from Italy and they all spoke in very loud Italian, leading to great confusion about our cues. It was all dubbed (badly) afterwards into English and I do wonder if it might have made more sense to American audiences if it had been left in Italian, or perhaps Double Dutch?

Our first day of shooting in San Francisco, down by the docks, was memorable in so much as we had terrible trouble closing off roads, and in fact any traffic control at all proved impossible. The director, Maurizio Lucidi, who was very, *very* Italian, made a call to the San Francisco Police Chief, who just so happened to be of Italian descent. The next morning we had police outriders escorting us to the location, with roads closed off all around and traffic officers all calling out, '*Ciao! Buon giorno*, Roger!' as we drove by. We enjoyed a very smooth shoot in the city after that.

ABOVE: Stacy Keach and I were a little bewildered by the fast-talking Italians involved in the making of *The Sicilian Cross*. I don't think either of us (or indeed the audience) really understood the plot!

While shooting in Rome I met up with Liza Minnelli, who was in town making a film with Ingrid Bergman called *A Matter of Time*, which her father, Vincente Minnelli, was directing. Liza had recently been in Mexico filming *Lucky Lady* with Gene Hackman and Burt Reynolds, and it appeared a few retakes had now been called for. Rather than wait for Liza to return to the US after completing her current project, the studio flew Gene, Burt and the director over to Rome for a few days. We all met for dinner one evening in a restaurant on the Via Veneto, and I'll never forget seeing the lone figure of Burt Lancaster sitting at the far end of the long dinner table that we'd been shown to. He didn't speak to, or acknowledge, anyone.

Towards the end of dinner, the 'curse of Rome' (otherwise known as the paparazzi) bundled their way through the door and started snapping. I'm not sure why, but all the actors immediately – almost instinctively – moved away from each other; not that there was anything going on, it just seemed to be a natural reflex to not be photographed with anyone else, thereby denying them a story.

At this point, Burt Lancaster now stirred into life. He placed his knuckles on the table and slowly raised himself to his full height. He slapped his left hand across his right forearm while pushing his clenched fist forward and upwards – the gesture is quite unmistakable in Italy. The paps did not need a second warning – they left, quickly, and we gazed with great envy at Burt.

Talking of Burt Lancaster, he did have a formidable reputation around the studios – apart from being a fine actor, he had one of the worst tempers in Hollywood. He had a well-known hatred of the press, and was invariably brusque and rude to them, once even resorting to physically throwing a hapless pap out of his hotel suite. But then he was well-known for being 'physical' on set, too.

In front of the cameras Burt was a force to be reckoned with and, though prized as an actor, he was often to be found in the middle of a major row or the cause of some disruption. When filming one of his most famous films, *The Birdman of Alcatraz*, he and director John Frankenheimer were almost constantly at loggerheads. Burt was always known as an actor who immersed himself in his roles and he reputedly became obsessed with the character of Robert Stroud, the real Birdman, researching his life and reading everything that was available on him. Apart from having the starring role, Burt was also co-producer on the film through his production company Hecht-Hill-Lancaster.

When shooting began, John Frankenheimer found Burt almost impossible to deal with – being the star and the money man made the director's job even trickier – and they argued about camera set-ups, dialogue, the lot. At one point, in an argument over where the camera should be placed for one particular scene, Burt physically picked Frankenheimer up and carried him across the set, depositing him where he thought the camera should go. Despite that treatment, Frankenheimer always admired the actor and they worked together again.

Michael Winner told me a great story about when he worked with the tempestuous Burt on a Western called *Lawman*. This was the early 1970s, at a time when Burt was at the height of his fame. In fact, such was his fame that Michael referred to his star as 'Mr Lancaster' throughout the whole shoot. But fame had not 'tempered' Burt's temper: one time they were filming a scene where Burt had to shoot his horse, drawing his Colt .45 to do the deed. In a later shot for the same sequence Burt used a rifle.

'Cut!' came the shout from the director's chair. 'Sorry, Mr Lancaster, but earlier you shot the horse with a Colt .45.'

Well, according to Michael, Burt went crazy, storming over to the director and shouting, 'What the hell do you know? I shot it with a Winchester! Why the hell would I use a Colt?!' With which he picked dear Michael up, carried him over to a nearby cliff and hung him over the edge, saying, 'So, *now* what did I shoot the fucking horse with?'

And Michael had to agree, 'You shot the horse with a Winchester, Mr Lancaster. Of course you did.'

❧

Back on the set of *The Sicilian Cross*, another memorable day (for all the wrong reasons) came when we moved to the south of Naples to shoot a sequence in a fish market. As I walked through the market, one of the fish vendors called out in Italian 'I have a fish for you', which was all part of the characters' secret codes. We first shot from behind the fish seller, over his shoulder on to me, with the crowd moving by behind. The cameraman, who seemed to be getting very agitated, kept cutting and asking us to go again, until, on the fourth take, he leapt up, scrambled over the ice and lunged at an old man behind me, hitting out at him and seemingly trying to beat him up.

'Whoah, whoah!' I cried. 'What are you *doing*?'

'Every time we turn the camera over, that old man comes into frame and starts jumping up and down, pulling faces behind you!' shouted the cameraman, as they started scuffling again. I couldn't stand it any more and asked that we move on to another shot. It was chaos, sheer chaos.

❧

In *The Wild Geese* I played Lieutenant Shawn Fynn and, along with my fellow officers, portrayed by Richard Burton, Richard Harris and Hardy Kruger, I had my own platoon to command and consequently the schedule offered me a few days off here and there, while the others were filming with their respective platoons. In my group was an actor called Percy Herbert who'd worked on a couple of episodes of *The Saint* and so I'd got to know him fairly well. One day, on our mutual day off, he came over and gave me some pages to read, saying it was his life story. It was absolutely fascinating.

During the Second World War, after just a few weeks' training, Percy was put on a ship and was told he was going to North Africa. However, midway, the orders were changed and the ship made its way to Singapore instead. No sooner had they arrived in the harbour than the Japanese air force struck from the air and their ship was sunk.

Meanwhile, the Japanese army advanced in over land, and as British guns were pointed out to sea, the rear action meant the Japanese very quickly won and occupied Singapore. Though wounded, Percy reached the shore with his pal and they were put into a British hospital where, after a few days, they heard gunfire, followed by screaming. Suddenly the doors to their twelve-bed ward were kicked open and two Japanese privates, machine guns at the ready, entered. Before they could open fire, a Japanese officer entered and with his cane knocked the soldiers' arms – and guns – down.

All the hospital patients were taken prisoner and Percy eventually ended up in Changi Prison as a prisoner of war. He, along with many other men from the jail, was then taken to work on the railroad that became the basis for the film *The Bridge on the River Kwai*.

In prison, Percy and his friend found that they were able to infiltrate the food stores in their camp and in their desperate need for sugar they took some, some of which they buried. When the theft was noticed, both Percy and his friend found themselves prisoners of the British who, for disciplinary purposes, ran a prison within the Japanese prison. For most of the time Percy found himself in British solitary confinement. There they were screamed

at, shouted at and everything was 'on the double', so poor Percy's feet never touched the ground. He had a terrible time and, ironically, all at the hands of the British.

ABOVE: It was back to South Africa, and the (then) Rhodesian border, for *The Wild Geese* – along with Richard Harris, Richard Burton and Hardy Kruger. And were we wild? No, of course not.

Throughout his internment Percy never received any mail from home and when the Australians finally liberated the camp he was handed a bundle of Red Cross envelopes. They were all from his fiancée, so before opening any he carefully put them in order of posted date. The first started, 'My Darling Percy', the second, 'My Dear Percy', but the third simply said, 'Dear Percy' and went on to say she had found a new love ...

On the troop ship home to the UK, Percy and his mate were so terrified of waking up in the night believing they were still prisoners of war and jumping over the side that they struck a deal whereby each night one would tie the other into his bunk. Such was the horrific toll of their imprisonment.

However, eventually they arrived at Liverpool docks and were given a pass to travel to London. Percy went straight to his mother's house and, after all these terrible years as a prisoner of war, walked down the basement steps, knocked on the door. His mother peered out.

'Blige me, Perce!' she said, adding, with typical British restraint, 'I'll put the kettle on!'

After a few days readjusting at home, Percy wanted to visit his old girlfriend's brothers, with whom he'd been great friends, and between them they arranged a meeting at Wood Green Underground Station. As Percy stood at the top of the escalator waiting, into his frame of vision came a female sergeant in the Auxiliary Territorial Service (ATS, the women's branch of the British Army in the Second World War) – his ex-fiancée. She told him that she had realized she'd made a huge mistake and that she had asked her brothers to set up this meeting between her and Percy. Happily, it wasn't long after that that they married. They went on to take up amateur dramatics together as a hobby and Percy later turned professional, which is how he came into my life.

When director David Lean was casting for his film *The Bridge on the River Kwai*, Percy was taken up to meet him at Film House in Wardour Street. Lean looked him up and down, and grunted, 'Not the type' before waving him out.

Percy, who had, not surprisingly, developed a nasty tic that came out when he was anxious or upset, a hangover from his mistreatment during the war, dived straight across the desk at Lean, face twitching like mad, 'Not the fucking type? What do you mean "Not the fucking type"? I was fucking there!'

'OK! OK! You're in the film!' said Lean.

When they arrived on location, David Lean got to hear Percy's whole story and asked him how the prisoners might have shown contempt to their captors. 'How would you do it so as you knew but the Japanese didn't?' asked Lean.

Percy said they'd whistle, and demonstrated with the tune 'Colonel Bogey', and that's how it came to be used in the film.

ꝏ

Just as Percy was an advisor on that film, we had our own advisor on *Wild Geese*. Colonel Mike Hoare – a well-known mercenary, also known as Mad Mike – used to give us pep talks, similar to those he gave to his men before a mission. He'd led mercenary groups in the Congo and was a formidable man to whom, it was said, Richard Burton's character of Faulkner paid more than an accidental resemblance. He and some of the ex-mercenary actors in the cast used to terrify me: one in particular would be talking to you and then, all of a sudden, you'd feel his bayonet at your throat and he'd say, 'That's how it's done, my son.'

In the film, Jack Watson played RSM Sandy Young. Jack was the son of music hall comedian Nosmo King, who took his name from sitting in a railway carriage – a 'no smoking' carriage. Over the years I made a few films with Jack, and he was a fine physical specimen of a man but took himself rather seriously, despite appearing in variety shows with his father and working on many comedy films in his early career.

Jack was always extremely nice, but could be very pompous at times. After tennis one Sunday, my make-up artist Paul Engelen, my hairdresser Mike Jones and I were sitting around the swimming pool relaxing and Jack stood on tiptoes at the edge of the pool, stretched his arms out and said, 'There's nothing like having your own pool, is there, Roger?' which rather annoyed the boys in the crew, to say the least.

He then did a perfect pike into the pool but his body stopped three feet into the water as he'd dived into the shallow end! His legs remained rigid, sticking out like the Eiffel Tower and not one person went over to see if he was OK, we just sat there laughing.

I'm ashamed to say that Jack's serious take on life was like a red rag to a bull with me. One morning on *The Sea Wolves* I had a word with our make-up artist Paul Engelen and when Jack slipped into the chair Paul proceeded to paint his face black.

'What's this for?' asked Jack.

'Oh, the director wants everyone made up for the night shooting and wants to run a camera test to see how everyone looks,' replied Paul.

Jack nodded knowingly, and sat bolt upright awaiting his transformation. An hour later, he reported on set, every bit the image of Al Jolson but minus the white lips. Andy McLaglen (our director) walked across with a look of total bemusement on his face.

'What the fuck are you looking like that for, Jack?' he asked.

I made good my exit, telling myself I really ought not to instigate these practical jokes.

Back on set with *The Wild Geese*, Richard Burton had some shoulder problems at the time and the script called for a long shot of his platoon in the bush, with Burton's character carrying President Limbani (played by Winston Ntshona). Derek Cracknell, our wonderful First Assistant Director, said to Burton that they could use his double for this particular shot. Jack Watson, who was also in the sequence, overheard and, realizing his principal was being doubled, wanted to know where *his* stand-in was.

Derek, sensing that there could be trouble brewing with Jack's somewhat misplaced feeling of self-importance, said, 'Jack, look at you and then look at all these herberts here. You're the perfect physical specimen, aren't you?'

Jack was forced to nod in agreement.

'Well, then. Which one of these herberts could *possibly* double you?'

Jack did the scene himself.

Being a cowardly actor, having to play heroes means I'm in no small way indebted to the stunt boys. Nosher Powell was the senior member of the Powell dynasty of stuntmen and in between film stunt work, he used to look after security at the Jack of Clubs, a club underneath the famous Isow's Restaurant on Brewer Street in Soho, which was run by Jack Isow's son.

One night Nosher said to him, 'This group that just came in, I think they're going to be trouble and we should get them out.'

'No, they'll be fine,' he assured Nosh.

Three or four hours later, a £500 bar tab had been run up and the group started to get up to leave. Remember, this was a few years ago and £500 was worth a lot more then. Nosher stood at the top of the stairs, 'Look, boys, you owe a heck of a lot of money and you're not leaving until you pay.'

'Oh yeah?' they said. 'Who's going to stop us, you and whose fucking army?'

'Just me and my dog.'

With that, Nosh pulled round his huge German shepherd dog, which was snarling and salivating at the end of a leash.

'Oh, and what's your dog gonna do, Nosh?'

'Well, when I say "attack", he attacks,' replied Nosher.

'Well, let's see then,' they goaded.

'Attack!' Nosher commanded. With that, there was a terrible sound of snarling and the crunch of bones, and blood squirted everywhere as dog tore trousers, ripping into the flesh beneath ... and poor old Nosh was flat on his back trying to push the damn thing off!

The gang, in hysterics, threw the £500 on top of Nosher, thanking him for the best laugh they'd had in years.

Speaking of stuntmen, one rather famous one whom I won't name … let's call him Roy … was late reporting on set at Elstree Studios one day for a sequence in an episode of *The Saint*. It turned out that he was on an adjacent stage, upstairs in a dressing room. In fact he was in the wardrobe peeping out as one of his fellow stuntmen gave the horizontal performance of *his* life with a young aspiring starlet. All the time this was going on, our assistant director was calling out, 'Roy! You're wanted on set! Roy!'

After reaching the inevitable conclusion, our intrepid hero waited a few moments before he made good his exit from the wardrobe and dashed down the stairs, five at a time, towards the stage where the call of 'Roy! Roy! We're waiting!' was becoming more and more audible around the entire studio. However, he missed his footing on the last stair, sprained his ankle and was unable to work for days. Voyeurism is not without its penalties!

I used to love spending time with the stunt boys, over dinner or a game of cards between set-ups. I always enjoyed hearing all their stories. One in particular that tickled me was of a card game organized when filming *El Cid*. Apparently one of the local boys had a terrible habit of slamming his hand of cards down with great force whenever he had a win. It rather annoyed the other boys, so the next day they decided to rig the table with charges and, when a winning hand was slammed down, the whole table went up in smoke.

There was another occasion I witnessed when I was on set with one of the elder statesmen of stuntmen. During breaks, he used to enjoy sitting in a chair and puffing on his old pipe and on this particular day he nodded off mid-puff. His kind and caring colleagues gently removed the pipe from his mouth, filled it with gunpowder and carefully placed it back. When he awoke from his slumber, he relit his pipe and there was the most almighty bang. Our friend's only reaction was to blow the cloud of smoke away, revealing his blackened face, and say, 'That tobacco's a bit fucking strong!'

My wonderful long-time stunt double and co-ordinator Martin Grace was quite probably the bravest man I ever knew. We'd worked together on about a dozen films and his easy-going Irish charm made him a firm favourite with everyone on the crew, though curiously nobody really ever got to know much about Martin himself. That's the way he liked it, I guess.

In October 2008 we met up at Pinewood for a reunion dinner centred around *The Spy Who Loved Me* and picked up the conversation just as though the intervening fifteen years hadn't occurred. There in the magnificent Pinewood Ballroom we met up with so many other Bond alumni, including director John Glen, writer Christopher Wood, stars Richard Kiel, Caroline Munro, Valerie Leon, Shane Rimmer and a host of wonderful friends from behind the camera. As I bade goodnight to Martin, I never for one moment thought it would be the last time I saw my super-fit friend.

Two years later, at his home in Spain, Martin was involved in a cycling accident that, on the face of it, seemed rather trivial compared to some of the great stunts he'd dared in my name, and indeed breaking almost every bone

RIGHT: My fearless stunt double and dear friend Martin Grace stood in for me in many of my outings as Jimmy Bond.

in his body on a train stunt in *Octopussy*, but there were (unknown) complicating factors and aged just sixty-seven Martin died in hospital.

I subsequently discovered – as did many of Martin's mates – that he had a daughter from a short-lived marriage. I know she was incredibly proud of her father too. In death Martin was, as in life, an enigma but one to whom I owe such a great debt – as he made this coward look like a hero.

❧

When tragic fatalities have happened while filming movies, canny producers have sometimes turned a disadvantage into quite the opposite in terms of publicity. For example, when Oliver Reed was filming *Gladiator* in Malta and, true to character, enjoying a few drinks in a local pub on his day off, he reportedly consumed liberal amounts of beer, suffered a massive heart attack and died. With most of his scenes in the can, the producers used a CGI mask on a double to complete the outstanding sequences and billed it as Reed's last film – and it was actually one of his best performances. A similar thing happened on *The Misfits* when Clark Gable died before shooting had ended, and though CGI wasn't around then, a body double was used.

Other actors who died mid-shoot and were doubled include John Candy, Bruce Lee, Heath Ledger and Donald Pleasence. A sense of morbid curiosity may have helped to fill seats, but ultimately I don't think any of their final films fared tremendously well – you just can't fake a star's power (or even double it) and that was certainly the case when, aged just forty-four, Tyrone Power dropped dead on the set of *Solomon and Sheba* in Madrid.

ABOVE: With the inimitable Elizabeth Taylor in my first movie in Hollywood, *The Last Time I Saw Paris*. Believe me, I was looking into the glass! *(REX/Moviestore Collection)*

BELOW: Two shots from *Diane* with Lana Turner. She taught me how to kiss with passion, but without the pressure. *(MGM/The Kobal Collection)*

ABOVE: With lovely Angie Dickinson in *The Sins of Rachel Cade*, 1961. Sadly I wasn't allowed to sin (on screen at any rate!). *(REX/SNAP)*

RIGHT: The poster for an 'intriguing' film … *The Sicilian Cross*, *The Executors*, *Opium Road*, *Street People*, it went by several titles and the poster was most definitely better than the film – though Stacy Keach was a delight.

LEFT: I recruited a few young starlets to help me find my missing halo on *The Saint*.

BELOW: In 1967 German magazine *Bravo* voted me the best television actor – naturally! – and their editor presented me with this lovely award.

ABOVE: (*Left*) Me 'persuading' dogs not to use this tree. (*Right*) We had attracted a big crowd for this set-up and had to stop Tony falling into the river by having someone clutch him from behind.

BELOW: The Aston Martin DBS from *The Persuaders!* sold for £545,000 at auction in May 2014 … wish I'd kept it now …

ABOVE: A shotgun wedding! With Lee Marvin and Barbara Parkins in *Shout at the Devil* in 1976, and that's Sir Ian Holm peering over the bride's shoulder. The black eyes were make-up – honestly!

BELOW: Not *Hart to Hart*, but with Stefanie Powers in *Escape to Athena*, going in for a close-up. My other co-stars included David Niven and Telly Savalas. The tagline on the poster was: 'The patriot, the professor, the comic and the stripper were fighting for what they believed in … GETTING RICH!' I couldn't have put it better myself!

ABOVE: They say an actor's life is a solitary one.
I say, 'nah, nah, nah-nah-nah' to that!

BELOW: Me looking well and truly goosed in a shot from *The Wild Geese*.
It's not all wine, women and song, you know.

ABOVE: At the Oscars in 1989 Michael Caine, Sean Connery and I presented the Best Actor in a Supporting Role award to Kevin Kline for his part in *A Fish Called Wanda* – and then tried to steal it off him.

BELOW: On a holiday in Venice with my old friend Bryan Forbes.

ABOVE: Tony Curtis with his wife Jill, Kristina and myself met up at the *Empire* Awards in London in 2006, where Tony picked up a much-deserved Lifetime Achievement Award.

BELOW: Kristina always threw the best birthday parties for me, this one at Le Dome on Hollywood's famous Strip. (*l to r*) Frank Sinatra, Joan Collins, Gregory Peck and my darling, at one of them.

ABOVE: With Frank and Barbara Sinatra and Chief Abbot William B. Williams (the American disc jockey who first called Frank 'The Chairman of the Board') at The Friars Club Man of the Year award in 1986. Believe it or not, I was that man!

BELOW: Dean Martin was always thought of as a hard-drinking rascal but in reality his glass was usually filled with apple juice.

LEFT: HSH Prince Albert II of Monaco presents me as a Monaco Goodwill Ambassador on behalf of the Ambassadors Club of Monaco in 2012, at the Hotel de Paris.

BELOW: (l to r) Kevin Costner, HSH Prince Albert II of Monaco, Kristina, myself and Sir Richard Branson at the Monaco Golf Club – we arrived by helicopter and left in Richard's hot air balloon!

RIGHT: Two of my favourite ladies: daughter Deborah and Kristina at the Cannes Film Festival in 2007 for *The Ladykillers*.

ABOVE: (*l to r*), my daughter-in-law Loulou and her husband Geoffrey (that makes him my son!), Deborah, me and Kristina with the lovely Geraldine and Michael Winner in Gstaad.

LEFT: My most recent film was *A Princess for Christmas*, during which three huge Bulgarian technicians fell on my leg – hence the attractive footwear in this cast shot.

ABOVE: With (*l to r*) Tore Wretman, HRH Princess Lilian (showing her sense of fun with that apron), Kristina and HM Queen Silvia of Sweden at a lunch party.

BELOW: (*l to r*) Lady-in-waiting Lena Luttichaü, HM Queen Margrethe II of Denmark and Pastor Peter Parkov, who married Kristina and me in Copenhagen. HRH The Prince Consort is not in the picture – because he took it!

RIGHT: My eldest son Geoffrey with his wife Loulou and daughters Ambra and Mia, with Kristina and me.

BELOW: (l) Kristina's daughter Christina with her horse Lucky. (centre) Kristina's son, Hans-Christian, his wife Henrietta and their two children Kathrine and Adrian.

ABOVE: (r) Kristina with her grandson Lucas.

LEFT: My youngest son Christian with his wife Lara, daughter Jessie and sons Tristan and Maximillian.

ABOVE: In 2011 the Royal Albert Hall staged a festive treat in aid of UNICEF – and here I am, with my daughter Deborah, introducing Captain Beaky and His Band, and a number called 'The Grasshopper'. (*Christine Goodwin/courtesy of RAH, 2011*)

LEFT: In 2012 I was awarded an Honorary Doctorate of Arts from the University of Hertfordshire. Their Chancellor, the Marquess of Salisbury, kindly presented it to me.

Kristina and me on a recent UNICEF trip to Aachen, Germany, and the Opening Ceremony of the World Equestrian Festival, looking rather regal in our carriage. (*Henry Herrmann/UNICEF*)

Tyrone's wife, Deborah, had asked the director King Vidor to ease the schedule but after a prolonged sword-fight scene with George Sanders, wearing heavy robes and working with real Roman swords that weighed fifteen pounds, on an elevated staircase landing, Sanders wasn't pleased with some of the shots and asked that the scene be shot over. Finally, after the eighth take, Tyrone said he could stand no more and threw down his sword.

'If you can't find anything there you can use, just use the close-ups of me,' he said angrily. 'I've had it!'

A short time later, after complaining of being tired and feeling pain in his arm, Tyrone was rushed to hospital, where he died within the hour. Tyrone Power had filmed seventy-five per cent of his scenes and, in order that the film could be completed, was replaced by Yul Brynner – who had to wear a wig.

Perhaps the most exploitative of all stories, and one which did curiously benefit the project, was when director Ed Wood filmed just a couple of minutes of silent footage of Bela Lugosi wearing a cape for a planned vampire project that never came to fruition. After Lugosi died, Wood decided to use the footage in *Plan 9 from Outer Space* and edited it into his movie multiple times. A body double, Tom Mason – who looked absolutely nothing like Lugosi – was brought in to finish the film. Totally nonsensical, the film is regarded as one of the worst films ever made, though ironically it's now a cult classic.

CHAPTER 5

The Good Guys (and a Few Rascals)

WHEN I LOOK BACK OVER MY LIFE I CAN'T QUITE BELIEVE I've counted some of my childhood acting heroes as being friends, co-stars and drinking buddies. I suppose I first met Gregory Peck sometime in the early 1970s, at the home of David Niven on Cap Ferrat in the South of France. They had been friends for years and Greg (along with his lovely wife, Veronique) became one of my dearest friends.

Greg had been a huge star from the 1940s and of course won the Academy Award for his role in *To Kill a Mockingbird* in 1962. As is often the way in this business, by the mid-70s leading roles in big films were not coming his way, but then he was cast in a fairly modest British-made horror film called *The Omen*. My dear old pal, publicist Jerry Pam, handled PR for the film, though ironically the studio told Jerry not to focus on Greg as they didn't think he was 'box office' enough; so instead Jerry centred his campaign around the sign of the beast

LEFT: Good guy or rascal? You decide. Robert 'Bobbie' Newton in one of his most famous roles as Long John Silver in *Treasure Island*.

ABOVE: Gregory Peck and David Niven were two very dear friends to me.

– '666'. It was massively successful, the film became box-office dynamite, and Greg's star shone brightly once again, leading to terrific roles in *The Boys from Brazil* and then *The Sea Wolves* with yours truly.

While making *The Omen*, Greg rented fellow actor Michael York's house in Belgravia and one evening I went for dinner there. As I said, it was the mid-70s and at the height of the IRA attacks on London, and when I left, around midnight, I found Greg outside on his back, having crawled underneath my car, thoughtfully checking if there was a bomb.

That kindly heroic deed certainly fitted in with roles he

played. Mind you, he wasn't averse to playing against type every now and again, as confirmed to me at a dinner one evening hosted by another pal, Johnny Mills. Fellow guest Laurence Olivier said, 'Amazing man, Greg. Doesn't worry about his image by playing a Nazi ...' They'd just worked together in *Boys from Brazil* in which Greg played the evil Nazi, Dr Josef Mengele.

Anyhow, in *Sea Wolves* Greg was to play British officer Colonel Lewis Pugh, and worked with a dialogue coach, the same one from *Boys from Brazil* I believe, to perfect his accent. He was a very meticulous actor and extremely well

BELOW: Greg, always handsome and debonair, was one of the kindest people I've ever known.

prepared, and though I later read somewhere that Greg felt insecure about his British accent in this film, well, all I can say is I was not aware of it. It was a super film directed by Andrew McLaglen, produced by Euan Lloyd and co-starring David Niven, Trevor Howard and, initially, Diana Rigg; but, alas, it didn't work out for one reason or another, and happily Barbara Kellerman took on her proposed role of Mrs Cromwell.

Of course, during the shoot, we all socialized frequently in Goa and New Delhi, and very pleasant it was, too. In fact, we all had bungalows in the compound of Fort Aguada and would dine at one or the other each evening. Greg was joined by Veronique, and they were the most compatible couple ever, totally adoring of one another. It wasn't an easy location, mind, as the heat was quite often unbearable. Our big relief after a day's shooting was to immerse ourselves in the Indian Ocean.

We had New Year's Day off and director Andy McLaglen and I ventured to the ocean early, I guess around 9 a.m. Having lain in the sun for a few minutes, Andy got up and stretched out his 6' 7" frame. He turned to me and said, 'Rog, I think it's time we hit the drink.' (Meaning went for a swim.)

At that very moment, Trevor Howard appeared as if from nowhere and, overhearing, said, 'Good idea! Do you think we can get a waiter down here?'

In actual fact, contrary to popular opinion, the Trevor I knew wasn't really the 'hell-raiser' the newspapers described him as. A great cricket lover as well as being entirely devoted to his wife, Helen, Trevor undoubtedly loved a drink but he was in fact rather a quiet drinker on the whole, preferring to have a longer session in the corner of a pub, with a few friends. Things could get a little noisy when the 'Howard Roar' went up, though. He always said, 'I don't raise hell, amigo, I just like to enjoy myself.' And he really did.

However, having said all that, Trevor loved life to the full and was always open to new experiences, not wanting to miss out on anything. Which is why he was led, along with show business reporter Bill Hall, to Pamplona to run with the bulls. This was in 1972, and Trevor was no spring chicken at the time – he was fifty-six years old. Perhaps

BELOW: With the inimitable Trevor Howard pointing out the location of the nearest bar, on a beach in Goa while filming *The Sea Wolves*.

One of my favourite photographs, featuring three of my favourite people.

he could be forgiven for having a few stiff drinks on this occasion.

The story goes that he'd been attending a film festival some miles away from Pamplona and seen that the world-famous bull run was taking place. After a few drinks with Bill Hall one night, Trevor suddenly announced that he wanted to do the run, and asked Hall to join him. Several hours later the two found themselves in Pamplona's main square – still the worse for wear after several Bloody Marys – along with 2,000 other runners, waiting for the beasts to be let loose. Having seen this event several times on the TV, I can't imagine what they were thinking of, but come the time, they set off running, given a head start before the bulls were released. After a few minutes, out of breath, Trevor slowed to a walk, with the crowds lining the streets and Bill Hall urging him on to keep running.

Suddenly the bulls appeared round the corner, thundering down the street at full pelt. Trevor, deciding enough was enough, tried to get over the barrier at the side of the road but got his leg stuck and simply had to cling on for dear life as the bulls charged past, missing them both but mowing down others in their wake. Luckily, both Trevor and Bill escaped unscathed and made their way to the nearest bar.

Good old Trevor!

⚜

John Mills, that rather straight-laced, fine English hero of many a war film and Knight Commander of the Order of the British Empire, had a rather unique party trick, which extended to most film sets he worked on – not least in the cosy tents during the making of *Scott of the Antarctic* – where

ABOVE: With Johnny Mills and Lady Mary at Johnny's eightieth birthday party at the St James's Club on Sunset Boulevard, along with Dudley Moore and his wife Brogan Lane.

he would drop his trousers, bend over and let off the most furious fart you can imagine but – as if that wasn't enough to impress – he would have a naked flame on standby and would ignite said anal wind to the great merriment of all around.

In the 1960s I was asked to become chairman of the Stars Organisation for Spastics (SOS, now SCOPE) but when I started playing Bond it became apparent, in 1977, that I would have to leave the UK if I wasn't to pay ninety-eight per cent tax on my salary: an actor's life in the spotlight is short, so we need to look after our pennies, and that's why

I decamped to Switzerland with its lovely snow-capped tax benefits. I therefore realized I would have to cut back on a lot of my UK commitments, SOS being one.

The committee asked if I had any ideas who could step in to replace me and I suggested Johnny Mills. He joked as the 'new boy' coming in he was actually a lot older than the outgoing chairman, but that was nothing new as I was older when I took over Bond from Sean Connery. Cheek!

Johnny and I were near neighbours in the UK in the 1970s, when he lived, with his wife Mary, in a house previously owned by the film mogul Alexander Korda and his one-time wife Merle Oberon. (I actually appeared in an episode of a TV drama series with Miss Oberon called *Assignment Foreign Legion*, which was not filmed on location in the desert, oh no, but at Beaconsfield Studios in rural Buckinghamshire. Mind you, I never actually met Miss Oberon as she filmed her bits elsewhere. Bit of a pointless digression really, but I do like to name drop when I can.)

Anyway, back to the story. One day in 1976 I suggested John and Mary join my then wife and me for dinner at a rather upmarket dining pub in Denham – you know, the sort of establishment where you pay a small fortune for steak and chips. I think it's fair to say Johnny probably hadn't eaten at this establishment since his recent ennoblement by the Queen.

The headwaiter welcomed us warmly, 'Ah, Mr and Mrs Mills ... and Mr and Mrs Moore ... let me show you to a nice table.' He then proffered some menus. 'Would you care for a drink first, Mrs Mills? ... And you, Mr Mills?'

'Tonight, Mr Mills, I would recommend the T-bone ... Oh, and Mrs Mills, the Dover Sole is absolutely beautiful ...' The friendly waiter probably said 'Mr Mills' and 'Mrs Mills' a couple of dozen times over the course of the dinner, just as he did 'Mr Moore' and 'Mrs Moore'. Until Mary snapped, that is.

'It is SIR John and LADY Mills,' she hissed through clenched teeth.

Johnny's head dropped down towards his dessert bowl and he said, quietly, 'Well, I have waited long enough for it!'

Some years later, at Johnny's eightieth birthday party in LA's St James's Club, Mary beckoned me over and asked, 'Who is that man sitting over there, I know the face but I just can't place him?' I told her it was Omar Sharif, to which she looked at me rather vaguely. Anyhow, I was invited to say a few words and, after congratulating my host on his four score years, told the assembled company that Johnny owed most of his career to being the only actor in England who could stand full height in a submarine. Cue much laughter – except from the direction of Mary who looked at me decidedly more vaguely than ever!

I know when to make good my escape.

Johnny died in April 2005, aged ninety-seven, and I attended his funeral along with many of his closest friends and family: Lord Attenborough, Stephen Fry, Leslie and Evie Bricusse, Anita Harris, Dame Helen Mirren, Dame Judi Dench, Jack Hawkins' widow Doreen and even Cherie Blair. Dickie Attenborough, moved to tears, spoke for us all when he said, 'We shall miss him desperately. But we shall have him with us always in the deep love and unmatched joy that he has bequeathed to all of us.' It never stopped raining that day, and I believe they were actually tears from heaven.

⧆⧆⧆

PREVIOUS PAGES: The cast of *The Sea Wolves*. This photograph includes so many old friends – it makes me smile every time I see it.

Back on the set of *Sea Wolves*, Greg Peck and I often chatted over a drink at the end of the day, and one evening I realized we'd both worked with John Huston – as an actor in my *Sherlock Holmes in New York* and as a director helming *Moby Dick* in which Greg had starred.

'Didn't like him,' said Greg, taking me aback a little, as I found Huston to be the consummate professional and a joy to work with.

'As a director,' continued Greg, 'all he cared about was getting the shot. In the scene where I was tied to the model of the whale in the tank at Elstree Studios and the waves were crashing all around me, Huston gave various instructions to lower the model into the water, and each time he held it there for longer than I could reasonably hold my breath. I was furious – he nearly drowned me.'

On another evening we were chatting about *Roman Holiday*, that great romantic movie Greg had made with Audrey Hepburn in 1953. In the final scene where Greg's character has to say goodbye to Audrey's Princess Ann, knowing it's the last time he'll ever see her, Greg said he felt it was going to be a hugely emotional scene and one that he was not going to hold back on. As the tears of sadness ran down his cheeks, the director William Wyler leaned across and said, 'No, Greg, don't get upset. Get angry! Angry! Angry!'

And that's how Greg was forced to play the scene – angry that he wouldn't be seeing his love again. He said it was one of the defining moments of his career and he realized just how important listening to a director like Wyler could be.

Oh, before I forget, I must mention a scene in *Sea Wolves* that I shared with the lovely Barbara Kellerman. It's the part where my character discovers that she is in fact a Nazi spy – though not before taking a bullet in my arm. The script called for me to change jackets, wrap a bandage around my bloodied and wounded arm, with blood running down into the palm of my hand, and go to the ball, which was being staged as a grand diversion for the attack on the German ships in the harbour. I went off to make-up and, as I was sitting in a chair waiting for my call, the Indian unit nurse came in, took one look, and said 'Oh my goodness! You have been injured!' and proceeded to attend to my fake wound. I don't think she'd ever worked on a film before.

I wish I'd been able to make more films with Greg and seen him more often, but sadly our geography placed us on different continents. I remember we did go fishing together once, off Cap Ferrat. We chartered a boat and forged our way out beyond the headland looking for signs of any water-propelled creatures. Having not caught so much as a herring, the captain called on the radio to other fishing boats in the area and they reported nothing in sight either. We then saw the reason: about sixty feet from us an enormous whale poked its nose up out of the water, obviously happy after its huge breakfast of fish.

Other places we used to hang out together were Crescendo and Ciro's nightclubs on Sunset Strip, where I saw Don Rickles perform a few times. Don took great enjoyment from insulting his audience – in fact he was known as an 'insult comic' – particularly the more prominent famous people in the audience. One night, I was there at one table,

Gary Cooper was at another and opposite him was a Mafia boss. Rickles began giving Cooper hell, then he turned his attention to me and then to the Mafia guy, saying the most terrible and goading things. But he always capped it off by saying, 'I'm only joking, sir, I'm only joking, sir.' And then, 'I'm now going to walk among you and squeeze venom all over you!'

He once said of Frank Sinatra, 'When you enter a room, you have to kiss his ring. I don't mind, but he has it in his back pocket.'

One time a group of us were at Frank's weekend house, relaxing by the pool, and Don started on Gregory Peck. It was the usual wisecracking routine, 'Who picks your clothes, Greg – Stevie Wonder?' and so on. For the most part, Greg took it in good humour but later that night Don went a step too far with a wisecrack and Greg leapt to his feet.

'Shall we step outside and settle this like gentlemen?' he challenged.

'I'm only joking, sir! I'm only joking,' Don guffawed.

The next day, Greg's wife Veronique had her white fluffy dog draped around her shoulders, like a stole, and we were all sitting in cast-iron chairs having lunch on the terrace. Again, Don started on Greg.

'When actors get old like you, Greg, they get mouths like flounders and can pull their lower lip over their forehead,' he said. As he spoke, Don moved his chair, and the grating of iron against the tiled floor startled the dog, which leapt off Veronique's lap and right under Rickles' chair, getting snagged between the floor and chair leg as it did so. It let out such a cry. Greg placed his cutlery down, signalled to his wife and they both stood up, picked up the dog, and went home. He simply couldn't take any more.

Other times, Greg and I played tennis or poker, or sat around telling jokes over a Jack Daniels or two. Whenever Kristina gave me a birthday party at Le Dome in West Hollywood, on what is called The Strip, Greg and Veronique were always the first to arrive and we picked up our conversation as though the intervening months had never occurred. I remember on one occasion at the end of the 1990s, Greg said he'd wound back on film work and was greatly enjoying taking his 'pony and trap' around theatres, whereby he'd sit on a stage and tell stories from his life and career. I always remembered the phrase 'pony and trap' and when I was invited to take part in a small tour in 2012 to help promote my last book, *Bond on Bond* (copies still available in all good book shops), I thought of Greg, and readily accepted. I took my pony and trap out again in 2013 – who'd have thought this boy from Stockwell would become not only an author, but a raconteur with his own stage show? I'll keep going until they find me out!

⁂

Our mutual friend, David Niven, was a happy constant in much of my life, and I shared many dinners with him over the years and played audience to his wonderful stories. Of course, we all knew most of them were exaggerated, borrowed or downright lies – but he told them so well. I remember one such story about how Errol Flynn and he (along with Niv's new girlfriend) went out boating one day from LA.

Miles offshore in the Pacific Ocean they started waterskiing (according to Niv he had introduced the sport to America!) and Flynn decided to cut Niv free and sailed off so that he could get to know the girl for himself. Niv then told us how, with only two skis for buoyancy, he swam miles back towards the shore – pursued by sharks if you please – until he was rescued by Ronald Colman.

Well, another one of those 'is it quite true?' stories came when Niv shared a house in Malibu with notorious bad boy Errol Flynn, which they called 'Cirrhosis by the Sea'. One of their regular visitors was the actor John Barrymore, who used to sit in his favourite chair and smoke his pipe, looking out on to the ocean. By all accounts, after John Barrymore died he was taken to the Utter McKinley Funeral Directors store on Sunset Strip, which had a clock with a long swinging arm in the window ominously counting down time.

One evening, Niv and some friends broke in and retrieved the body, took it home, sat it in Barrymore's favourite chair … and awaited Errol's return home!

Flynn's book, *My Wicked, Wicked Ways*, was going to be made as a film by Roy Huggins, who was a producer at Warner Bros during my contract years there, and Roy wanted me to play Flynn. Alas, Errol had what you might best say was a 'difficult' relationship with Jack Warner, the famed studio head, stemming from the time when one of Jack's brothers suffered a heart attack after a big argument with Flynn. One day shortly afterwards, Jack walked into the dining room of the studio and noticed a new English writer who had joined the staff who had an uncanny resemblance to Flynn.

'Get that son of a bitch out of here!' Jack exploded. 'He looks like Flynn!'

'But it's not Flynn,' someone said.

'I don't care! He *looks* like Flynn. Get him out!'

I probably didn't help matters myself when I was called in for a meeting with old Jack Warner to discuss the role.

'I understand Roy wants you to play Errol Flynn?' said the great man.

'Yes, it's a part I'd love,' I replied.

'I also understand he calls me a thief in his book?'

'Well, aren't you?' I asked.

'Son of a bitch – I won't make the movie!'

Meeting over.

I only met Errol Flynn once – when I was understudying David Tomlinson and Geoffrey Toone in *The Little Hut*. David was going out with a girl who he knew had been in a relationship with Flynn some years earlier, so on hearing Flynn was coming to town, David thought he'd have a little fun with his love and faked a telegram:

'Darling. Am coming to London. Let's pick up where we left off. Love Errol.'

It didn't take long for the young lady to twig it was Tomlinson who had sent it, and she told Flynn about the gag when he landed in town.

'I'll fix the son of a bitch,' said Flynn.

Flynn was a huge, tall, very imposing man and he arrived at the Lyric Theatre Shaftesbury Avenue, just in time to stand in the wings with his sleeves rolled up for when David glanced in his direction ... and Flynn was glaring at him wildly. Terrified, David couldn't get his lines out for the next five minutes!

Charmer though he undoubtedly was, Flynn also loved to fight – and I mean fists flying, down and dirty, slugging it out. In fact, he loved fighting to such an extent that he was often to be found sparring with a professional fighter, just to keep himself in shape.

Another legendary slugger was the director John Huston, and the story goes that one night, fed up and bored at yet another Hollywood party, Huston and Flynn decided to retire to the garden and knock seven bells out of each other. They were on good terms, there was no issue between them, they just wanted a fight. So for a goodly part of the rest of the evening, the other guests were treated to the sounds of the pair of them, toe to toe, knocking each other around the garden – at the end of which they both wound up in hospital for repairs!

⁂

Another great actor with a fondness for the bottle was Robert Newton, who was a wonderful Bill Sikes in *Oliver Twist* as well as an unforgettable Long John Silver in *Treasure Island*. Legend has it he once walked the length of the corridors at Denham Studios with his honourable member for Wapping hanging out while under the influence.

Newton had an unfortunate way about him when sloshed, and while making a film with Herbert Wilcox and Anna Neagle he upset them in a way only Newton could. Later that day he got a call from his agent saying that unless he turned up the next morning sober, on time and apologized, he'd be fired.

At 8.30 a.m., Wilcox and Neagle appeared on set and Newton was nowhere to be seen, but suddenly they heard him coming down from the gantry, rather unsteadily, on a ladder.

'I am told that I have to apologize to you both for my unseemly behaviour yesterday, well I'd love to but am afraid I cannot.'

With that he walked off the set and out of the picture.

I remember one time when I was in LA with my then wife, Dot Squires, Trevor Howard phoned from the Beverly Hills Hotel and said he was with Newton.

'Bobby, come here,' said Trevor. 'I want you to speak to Dorothy Squires, a great artist!'

Bobby came on the phone and slurred, 'Madam, I admire all your paintings.'

There's one more story about Bobby Newton that always makes me smile. He was appearing in a play in London's West End and towards the end of the run one Saturday night the curtains didn't rise. The audience was getting more than a little restless when suddenly there was a commotion behind the curtain and a pair of shoes appeared at the base. The audience went quiet, the curtain parted and Bob's face appeared through it.

'Ladies and gentlemen!' cried the star. 'The reason this curtain hasn't risen is because the stage manager has the fucking impertinence to suggest that I am pissed!'

❧

One actor I've always admired – in fact I've always been a little envious of – is Peter O'Toole, as I would have dearly loved to have played Lawrence of Arabia. I wouldn't have been anywhere near as good as him mind, and I did get to know him later.

Michael Caine once told me a story of when he was cast to understudy O'Toole in the play *The Long and the Short*

and the Tall at the Royal Court Theatre, in London. One Saturday night after the show O'Toole invited him to a restaurant. Eating a plate of egg and chips was the last thing Michael says he remembered, before he woke up in broad daylight in a strange flat.

'What time is it?' he asked O'Toole, holding his aching head in his hands.

'Never mind what time it is! What fucking *day* is it?' came the reply from a similarly slumped O'Toole.

It turned out to be five o'clock on Monday afternoon – and the curtain was set to go up at eight. They rushed to the theatre, where the stage manager told them the restaurant owner had been in and had banned them from his establishment – for life. Michael was about to ask what they'd done when O'Toole whispered, 'Never ask what you did. It's better not to know …'

O'Toole was legendary for his boozing and that probably wasn't helped when in his first film, *Kidnapped*, he starred alongside Australian actor Peter Finch – an even mightier drinker, if that were possible.

Shooting in Ireland, they were refused a drink because it was after closing time, so the stars decided to buy the pub and wrote out a cheque there and then. After an all-night drinking session, and having sobered up a little, they later rushed back to the pub and were mightily relieved the landlord hadn't cashed the cheque.

By all accounts O'Toole and Finchie remained friends

LEFT: I always admired Peter O'Toole; legendary boozer he may have been but he was also a legend in front of the camera and a good dancer by the looks of things.

with the publican and when he died his wife invited them to his funeral. Both men sobbed loudly at the graveside, and an overcome Finchie eventually had to turn away ... only for his face to change from one of sadness to one of confusion as he realized they were at the wrong funeral – their friend was being buried 100 yards away!

⋘⋙

Richard Harris had a fairly well-earned reputation as a hell-raiser – he certainly lived life to the maximum, that's for sure. I first became aware of his 'personality' when I was making *The Saint* at Elstree. Harris was over at Pinewood shooting a film called *The Heroes of Telemark* with Kirk Douglas.

The director, Anthony Mann, had originally been signed to direct *Spartacus* some years earlier but he and Kirk Douglas didn't get on, and so Mann was replaced by Stanley Kubrick. Mann had also previously worked with Richard Harris and they didn't get along too well either, so bringing them all together wasn't perhaps the best of ideas.

Kirk Douglas and Richard Harris were very jealous of each other and were constantly arguing about who the 'star' was. I remember my friend, publicist John Willis, telling me that their demands became increasingly ridiculous – to the point of seriously affecting the production. For instance, Harris rolled up at the studio one day with a tape measure, measured Douglas's trailer and then announced he was going home – apparently it was a few inches bigger than his – leaving the cast and crew with nothing to do until a longer trailer was found and brought to the studio. On another occasion, Kirk Douglas fired his chauffeur after an argument and Richard Harris immediately turned round and hired him.

Doris Spriggs – who went on to become my personal assistant for twenty-nine years – worked on *Heroes* in the production department and told me that they were nearly run out of town when they were filming on location in Norway at a lovely old Norwegian church. The church had survived the worst ravages of World War II, only to be burned to the ground by the English film crew when an arc light overheated after being left on overnight. Compounding matters further, all the extras marched through the town dressed in full Nazi uniform thinking nothing of the effect it might have on the elderly inhabitants, who were convinced the Reich had risen once more.

Things got worse between the two stars when they moved on location to Rome, and one evening attended a film premiere there. Earlier in the day, the British papers ran a story about all the childish behaviour and petty rivalry between them, and Harris was understandably furious. When he saw John Willis in the foyer of the cinema, he pushed everyone else out of the way and demanded to know who leaked the story. John said nothing so Harris threatened to hit him, and would have done had they not been pulled apart.

But then, ironically, on the last day of shooting back at Pinewood, both Douglas and Harris were in the corridor walking towards each other – a bit like the scene from *High Noon* – and John Willis found himself right in between them. 'I couldn't believe my eyes,' John said to me. 'As they met, they shook each other's hands like they were old friends and walked off to their dressing rooms!'

In the late 1960s, Richard Harris divorced his wife Elizabeth, and afterwards Elizabeth sent him a bird in a silver cage, with the message, 'Here's one bird that will never get away.' In turn, he sent her an antique cowbell saying: 'Wherever you go, I'll now be able to hear you.'

⚜

I always try to help out an old friend where I can, and such was the occasion when Rex Harrison called me one day to ask a favour. Rex was starring in a play in Oxford in 1969 and couldn't therefore attend the London premiere of *Staircase* – a film he had made with Richard Burton – so he asked if I would escort his then wife, Rachel Roberts. I agreed and duly arrived at the Connaught Hotel, where she was staying, and called up to her room to say I was ready with the car.

'Come up to the room, darling,' said Rachel.

Conscious of time, I went upstairs and found the door open, and there inside stood Rachel in her petticoat – one breast hanging below her brassiere and the other above – with another lady in the room, sipping champagne.

'Come in and have a drink, darling!'

'No, no, Rachel, I'll wait in the bar,' I said, making a hasty escape from what I thought might turn into a sticky situation. After what seemed like an age, she came down, I leapt up and bounded across to the door.

'Time for another drink?' she asked.

'We really ought to go, Rachel.'

'Nonsense! There's always time for another drink, darling,' she said, dragging me back to the bar.

Eventually we got away from the hotel and drove to the premiere. When we pulled into Haymarket, where the premiere was being held, a whole horde of photographers converged around the car as I opened the door for Rachel to step out.

ABOVE: Rex Harrison and Rachel Roberts – there were always fireworks when these two were involved.

'Here, get a picture of my boyfriend!' she yelled. 'I'll make you famous, Roger!'

I rather hurriedly pushed my inebriated friend into the theatre, just as she screamed, in her strong Welsh lilt, 'Are they 'ere?' She wasn't referring to the Royal party, which, in this case, was Princess Margaret, but rather to the Burtons – Richard and Elizabeth were due to attend.

'No,' I said, as I hushed her from screaming further and pushed her through to our seats in the dress circle. After a few minutes, Richard and Elizabeth arrived and the Grenadier Guards started playing music. At almost the same moment, Princess Margaret arrived at her seat and, before I could restrain her, Rachel shouted, 'I've got to say hello to my Richard!' and, with that, clambered over everybody, including Her Royal Highness, much to Burton's great embarrassment.

She returned to her seat, grumbling under her breath and humming along to 'We'll Gather Lilacs In The Spring', kicked her shoes off, put her feet up on the balustrade in front, and continued chuntering about how 'Richard cut me dead'. I explained he was in company with HRH and we really ought to settle down for the film.

No sooner had the film started than I heard a gentle snoring coming from next to me and thanked goodness she'd fallen asleep. However, minutes later, there was a sudden and very loud cry, and Rachel sat bolt upright.

'The bastards! They cut the close-up of my lovely Rex!' she exclaimed.

Never had ninety minutes seemed so much an eternity as that evening, and afterwards we all went to the Savoy for the party. As any dutiful star/host would, Richard (with Elizabeth) stood at the entrance to receive all the guests and, as I went through, Burton whispered, 'Good luck, boyo,' in my ear.

When the Toastmaster called for everyone to 'Be upstanding' as HRH entered, Rachel said, 'I'm not bloody getting up!' I dragged her to her feet, saying, 'You will!' through my clenched teeth, and really was beginning to regret ever accepting Rex's invitation.

Meanwhile, the dancing started and a waiter came to our table to say Rex was on the phone for Rachel. He'd just come off after his play, in which he was starring with Elizabeth Harris (ex of Richard Harris) and asked how Rachel was behaving. I was suitably diplomatic and gentlemanly – and then he asked to speak to Burton.

At this time, Burton was dancing with HRH, and so I quietly stood behind them and coughed politely to attract his attention.

'Oh, sorry, boyo, you want to dance with 'er? Be my guest!' he said as he pushed Princess Margaret towards me.

'No, no ... I mean yes, I would, Ma'am, but no ... Richard,' I said, 'Rex is on the phone and wants to speak to you.'

'Right-oh boy, look after things here, will you?'

I smiled politely ...

Rachel was a lovely lady and a wonderful actress, but a terrible handful. Rex was her second husband and she was Rex's fourth wife. Rachel always had a great aversion to sailing, but every year Rex chartered a boat in the Mediterranean and took Rachel's best friend with him for the trip – Elizabeth Harris ... Having discovered Rex's affair with Elizabeth, Rachel divorced him in 1971. She was devastated after the divorce, moved to the States and tried to carry on, but it was reported that her alcoholism and depression increased, eventually leading to her suicide in 1980, aged just fifty-three. It was terribly sad.

I continued to see Rex from time to time and he was always friendly towards me, apart from one day when I was staying with Leslie Bricusse in France. Rex had arrived (uninvited) two days earlier, after being besieged by the press at his house on Cap Ferrat following Rachel's death. Leslie explained I'd been promised the guest room and the screenwriter Jack Davies, who lived next door, suggested Rex went to stay with him.

We all joined up for dinner at a restaurant one evening and I guess there were about six of us. Throughout the evening I felt rather guilty about Rex having to move and I decided that the least I could do was to get the bill for dinner, at which Harry Belafonte and his wife and James Baldwin had joined us, at my invitation. When we had finished, I proffered my American Express card and Rex came up from behind me, tore the card from my hand and threw it on the floor.

'I don't want your damned plastic!' he shouted.

'But I want to get dinner,' I reasoned.

'No! I don't mind paying for YOUR friends,' he snapped.

The next morning I was having breakfast in a pagoda in the garden at Leslie's home, when Rex came across the lawn, sat down and looked at me. 'I'll get breakfast this morning ...' I said, with a smile.

Curiously, Rex and David Niven just didn't get on and Rex was always rather pissed off with Niv, saying, 'He's been on the Cap long before I arrived, yet he's never invited me for dinner or a drink.'

Rex could be a rather mean-spirited man, to put it mildly and, unfortunately, a lot of people in the business had been treated badly or spoken to nastily by him at some point or other, which was underlined when I joined Kirk and Anne Douglas, along with Greg and Veronique Peck, to see a play in LA one night. Claudette Colbert was co-starring in it with Rex. Afterwards, we went round to see Claudette and took her to dinner at Chasen's Restaurant. But we didn't ask Rex, I always felt a bit sniffy about that, but I'm afraid the Douglas's had no time for him. I never needed to ask why.

Rex's next wife was Elizabeth (Liz) Harris – she was the fifth of his six wives. I, of course, knew Liz through my sometime co-star Richard Harris, and she lived with Rex in a big house off Belgrave Square in London. She once told Richard (who told me) of their lifestyle. Rex would dress immaculately before taking the lift down from his bedroom to the first-floor dining room for breakfast. In fact, he'd take a good thirty minutes to dress, and would put on his cape and newly polished boots even if he was just popping to the corner to post a letter. After breakfast, he would call the butler in to discuss the wine list for lunch, then go upstairs to change, only to re-emerge a few hours later in his tweeds for his meal and to sample the wine. The shout would invariably go up, 'How dare you serve me corked wine!'

Rex always sent the wine back in restaurants – and is the only person I ever knew who did the same at home too.

The butler, in what must have been a well-worn and quite frustrating routine, would have to ensure there were buckets of ice available at 11.45 a.m. and 5.45 p.m. in three different rooms in case Rex wanted a drink in any one of them. He insisted Liz dress for dinner every night too, even if they were eating in alone, and was of the firm belief that children should be seen and most definitely not heard, which made life a little tricky for Liz and her three sons. It might not surprise you to hear the marriage was short-lived.

Rex wasn't regarded very warmly by those who knew him (or even knew of him) but I will say the one very decent thing he did do was look after my lovely friend Kay Kendall when she became ill. Kay and Rex had become an item in the mid-50s, when he was still married to Lilli Palmer, and when he discovered from her doctor that she was suffering from terminal myeloid leukaemia, he arranged a divorce from Lilli in order to marry Katie (as we all knew her) and care for her, on the understanding he'd remarry Lilli after Katie's death. In the event, Lilli was also having an affair with Carlos Thompson and married her lover, so she and Rex never got back together.

Rex kept the illness from Katie, who believed she was suffering from an iron deficiency, and cared for her until she died aged just thirty-two. He often said one of his greatest pleasures was to 'simply sit and admire Kay'.

Quite how Katie put up with him I'll never know, but when Rex was starring in *My Fair Lady* on Broadway she used to have to stand at the side of the stage for every performance when he sang 'I've grown accustomed to your face' as he point-blank refused to sing it to his co-star Julie Andrews, whom he hated with a passion. He in fact suggested the song should be dropped, but the producers wouldn't hear of it and so Rex said the only compromise would be if he could sing it to Kay.

Ironically, when he won the Oscar for the film version in 1964, he smiled widely as he dedicated it to his two fair ladies – Julie Andrews and Audrey Hepburn.

I got on very well with Peter Sellers and I knew three of his wives quite well, too. He was a solitary character though, always preferring to hide behind a mask, and consequently you never *really* got to know the real Sellers. This was, after all, the man who said, 'To see me as a person on screen would be one of the dullest experiences you could ever wish to experience.'

BELOW: Don't ask me why Peter Sellers was attempting to paint my toenails at Cubby Broccoli's house – I simply can't remember.

Although a star of comedy films, Peter very desperately wanted to be a romantic lead, though knew he wasn't classically good-looking. Sadly, he humiliated his first wife, Anne, when he told her about a great affair he was having with Sophia Loren, which was actually all in his head as there never was any romance with Sophia whatsoever. After divorcing Anne he met Britt Ekland at the Dorchester, as she was in London for a PR junket having signed a contract with 20th Century Fox. They married two weeks later. The marriage only lasted four years, as Britt couldn't live with Peter and his violent mood swings any longer. A couple of years later he married Miranda Quarry and, though I didn't go to the wedding, I was there for the honeymoon.

They were staying on the Cap Ferrat in the South of France, and I was staying at the same hotel while filming *The Persuaders!*.

One day Leslie Bricusse was bringing Johnny Gold around the Cap to the bay of Villefranche in his Riva and I was on Sellers' yacht. Sellers and I spoke with one of the customs patrol boats and, having supplied them with a few hundred cigarettes and a couple of bottles of Scotch, we suggested they pull Leslie over on the pretence of him coming into the bay too fast. From a safe distance aboard Sellers' yacht we cried with hysterics as their boat was indeed pulled over and we could see Leslie's face turning red with embarrassment as the officials produced this cargo of illicit contraband (supplied by us) from down below. Protesting his innocence, Johnny started waving a large white envelope around, which was addressed to Sellers from his London tailor.

'We're here to see Peter Sellers!' he shouted, evidently

hoping that this information would be enough to secure their release.

Finally, when we couldn't bear watching them any longer, we waved to the customs men to let the errant 'pirates' off. When they arrived on shore, Johnny gave the envelope to Sellers, who opened it only to reveal a big bag of some white powdered substance, together with a note saying it was a 'gift for the honeymoon'.

That's the closest I've ever come to being arrested, let me tell you.

That evening, back at the hotel, Sellers called us down to his room, and he was – shall we say – rather 'far gone' on the contents of his envelope, telling us his bed was a flying carpet and he was going to fly around the harbour – and asking if we would like to go with him ...

❧

Talking of things potent, one of Peter's good friends was Graham Stark. I worked with Graham on *The Sea Wolves* but he is most probably more fondly and famously remembered for his many appearances in the *Pink Panther* films with Peter, they were old mates and loved working together. In *The Pink Panther Strikes Again* Graham played an old Austrian innkeeper, and had the most wonderful – and often quoted – scene where Clouseau walked in to book a room and looked down at a little dog in the reception area.

'Does your dog bite?' asks Clouseau.

'No,' replies the old innkeeper, at which point Clouseau lowers his hand to stroke the 'nice doggie' and it attacks him.

'I thought you said your dog does not bite?!' exclaims Clouseau.

'That is not my dog,' replies the innkeeper.

Anyhow, filming the scene, director Blake Edwards announced, 'Graham, Peter and I think that you'd look good if you smoked a Meerschaum pipe when we do this scene.'

Graham had never smoked in his life, but happily agreed to go along with the request. The only problem being that they didn't load it with tobacco, but hash.

Graham dutifully puffed away on the pipe but every time he opened his mouth to speak, only gibberish came out. Edwards, Sellers and the entire crew couldn't stop laughing. Graham, meanwhile, thought it was the best day of his comedy life as he'd never had this amazing comedic effect on anyone before. Poor Graham.

❧

In later years, like me, Sellers lived in Gstaad and he had the most wonderful chalet there. After divorcing Miranda in 1974, he married a young actress named Lynne Frederick – she was twenty-three, he was fifty-two. Many of his friends felt that marrying the much-younger Frederick was a mistake and regarded her as an opportunist who married Sellers for his money. Just before his untimely death in 1980, Peter had made arrangements to see his lawyers to change his will and exclude Frederick, whom he was on the verge of divorcing. The night before he was due to sign the papers he suffered a massive heart attack and died, leaving Frederick, his widow, to inherit almost his entire estate, which was estimated at £4.5 million, plus all future royalties from his films.

Meanwhile, he left his children £800 each in a calculated and deliberate move to make them find their own way in life. It is thought that the feeling of rejection ultimately led to his son Michael's early death. Very sadly, Michael died at fifty-two, exactly twenty-six years after his father's death.

Of course, Frederick continued to profit from the estate and even sued Blake Edwards and United Artists, the producers of *Trail of the Pink Panther*, which was made after Sellers' death and used out-takes of the late actor. She was awarded $1.475 million in damages for 'insulting the memory' of her late husband.

After a very brief marriage to David Frost, she married a surgeon named Barry Unger, by whom she had a daughter, Cassie. Aged just thirty-nine, Frederick died in 1994, and her mother Iris inherited the estate until Cassie came of age. Which is how it came to pass that a person whom Sellers never knew now controls his estate and owns all of his belongings, while his own natural children remain disinherited.

As for my own experiences of Lynne Frederick? It was around 1977 or 1978 when Peter called me at my home in Tuscany, saying he was coming into the port nearby with his yacht and had Dr Christiaan Barnard (his heart surgeon, who had performed the first human heart transplant) and Lynne Frederick on board, and asking, 'Could we meet?'

I drove down to the port and found Peter leaning against a rail on the deck of his boat while Lynne was busy massaging his member, which in turn was popping out of his swimming shorts to say hello.

'Uh-oh!' I thought. 'She's trouble!' And I think I was right.

❧

Gstaad and *The Pink Panther* feature heavily in a story Victor Spinetti told me. Victor was the most wonderful raconteur and larger-than-life character. I first met him when he guest-starred in *The Saint*, though of course he more famously went on to appear in several of the Beatles' films – as he would often tell anyone who happened to be in earshot.

A year or two before I moved to the Swiss ski resort, Victor decamped there to film *The Return of the Pink Panther*, which my old friend Lord Lew Grade funded. Peter Sellers had been lured back to play Clouseau a decade after his last outing, due, no doubt, in part to him needing to re-establish his box office appeal following a few not very successful films. Victor had a few very funny scenes as a hotel worker, which left Peter in hysterics on set as it happens. A good thing, surely? No, I'm afraid not, as in the rushes screening Victor got more laughs from the crew than Peter did, and the editor was ordered to move in with his scissors.

Quite oblivious to this, Victor later accepted the invitation from Lew Grade to attend the star-studded premiere in Gstaad and to take part in the various press junkets. It was only when he arrived in Gstaad that he was told that most of his screen time had been left on the cutting-room floor. Meanwhile, all the posters in the town proclaimed welcome to the stars 'Peter Sellers, Christopher Plummer, Catherine Schell and Victor Spinetti' in huge four-foot-high lettering. Victor realized he could hardly back out and return to the airport, so he

RIGHT: Victor Spinetti was a fantastic raconteur. His fund of stories was legendary and he told them with great humour and warmth.

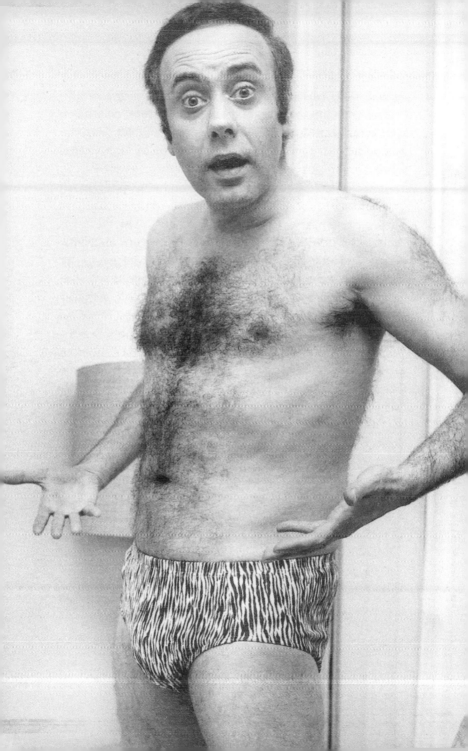

agreed to do whatever they wanted.

The one line Victor had left in the film was when Clouseau asked Victor's hotel manager character, 'Do you have a rheum?' and Victor responded with, 'A *rheum*?' That was it.

Dreading that the press might ask him how he prepared for his role in the film, Victor called his old mate Richard Burton, who was then also resident in Gstaad, with his sometime wife Elizabeth Taylor, and confided in them that he was feeling rather uneasy, particularly about having to attend the big post-film party afterwards, where he was sure he would feel a bit of a sham celebrating his role. Richard, having not been invited, decided that he and Liz would support their old friend by turning up and – of course – the photographers went mad. Peter Sellers' face dropped and Liz Taylor proceeded to wind him up even further by saying things like, 'Why did you choose *this* place for the party?' and 'What's that *awful* music the band's playing?' (it was 'The Pink Panther Theme') and so on. Then, director Blake Edwards introduced his wife, Julie Andrews, to sing, at which Burton leaned over to Victor and said, 'Anything you can do to follow, old love? The world's press are here and might discover you all over again.'

Victor suggested he could do his monologue of 'When Alec Guinness was fucked by the Turks', to which Burton enthusiastically agreed, and as soon as Julie Andrews completed her song, Richard stood to his feet and said, 'Ladies and gentlemen, and now my great friend Victor Spinetti ...!'

Sellers leapt up and shouted 'NO!'

Burton smiled, 'Of course, Peter, I'm sorry. Come, Victor. Come, Elizabeth,' and they swept out, only stopping momentarily for the blinding series of camera flashes.

'We'll get you in the bloody papers yet, Victor!' said Burton.

The next morning, Burton arrived at Victor's hotel to take him back home for lunch with Elizabeth. On the way back they picked up the European newspapers and found their three faces plastered across most of the front pages.

'Success!' cried Richard. Only on closer inspection they discovered the captions all read, 'At the premiere of *The Return of the Pink Panther* Richard Burton, Elizabeth Taylor and Mel Ferrer ...'

That's show business, folks!

CHAPTER 6

The Rat Pack

FUNNILY ENOUGH, I KNEW SOME OF THE *ORIGINAL* RAT Pack from the 1950s … David Niven was one, as were Frank Sinatra, Humphrey Bogart, Lauren Bacall, Swifty Lazar, Cary Grant and Rex Harrison among others. You see, it was a moveable feast then, 'visiting members' were allowed and the name was actually coined by the lovely Bacall when she gazed upon the very motley crew of revellers returning from a show in Las Vegas.

Niv told me the story that Frank Sinatra had invited a few friends to join him at the Desert Inn in Vegas, where Noël Coward was opening in a show. There were about fourteen of them, so they took the overnight train, in a private coach, of course, for the overnight trip. It was champagne and caviar all night. Next day, they partied in the day and then watched Coward's triumphant first night, before partying some more. This went on for four days and four nights, and I remember Niv remarking that towards the end of those four nights, Frank was the only member

LEFT: Dean Martin and Jerry Lewis in the early days. One of the greatest-ever comedy pairings.

of this merry band who seemed able to cope with it. It was at this point that Lauren Bacall made her famous remark, 'You lot look like a goddam Rat Pack!'

Humphrey Bogart was always hailed as the head of the Rat Pack, but Frank Sinatra was the President, and after Bogie's death he assumed the mantle. The Rat Pack continued to have a 'fluid' membership until the sixties, when it was used – by the press – to refer to Frank, Dean Martin, Sammy Davis Jr, Peter Lawford and Joey Bishop. I came to know Frank, Dean and Sammy in later years.

I first met Frank in the 1950s at a club called Moulin Rouge in Hollywood. I was then under contract to Warner Bros and was invited, as a very minor celebrity, to attend a Thalian Society charity fundraiser that was themed around 'Cowboys and Indians'. At the dinner, my first memory of Frank is of him having a rather public confrontation with the most famous cowboy of all, John Wayne. The unpleasantness stemmed from the fact that Jack Warner, the head of Warner Bros, bid $1,000 to have a Warner Bros contract artist, Gordon MacRae, sing at the event … only for John Wayne to bid $2,000 for him *not* to sing.

Frank felt The Duke had insulted his friend and made a point of it. Seeing the tall-framed Duke face up to Frank – who was a lot shorter, thinner and, with his gaunt cheeks, certainly appeared less formidable – was something I'll never forget.

But Frank stood up for his friends. He was fiercely loyal. That was just one of the qualities that endeared him to me.

There had been history between Frank and The Duke going back some years, but eventually they patched up their differences – enough that when an All-Star Tribute to the great Wayne was produced in the mid-70s, Frank

ABOVE: With two founder members of the *original* Rat Pack, talent agent Swifty Lazar and David Niven.

agreed to host the show. It's said that even The Duke was surprised to see Frank hosting, but the evening went well and the stars – including Maureen O'Hara, Jimmy Stewart, Lee Marvin, Angie Dickinson, Sammy, Bob Hope and the like – all shone bright. Towards the end of the show, after all the songs and tributes, John Wayne stole the show when he rose to address his guests, 'Tonight you've made an old man and an actor very happy. You are happy, aren't you, Frank?'

The night Frank and I met, we only really exchanged pleasantries. Frank greeted me warmly and said, 'Hi, I'm

Frank Sinatra,' as if I – or anyone else in that room come to that – didn't know who he was. His humility was another of his qualities that so impressed me. I thought this was a man I would like to meet again.

Francis Albert 'Frank' Sinatra's entry into this world had not been an easy one. For as long as I knew him, Frank continually said that he would like to meet and kill the doctor who delivered him. He had used forceps, which had badly damaged Frank's ear and scarred his face. Alarmed that the just-born infant was not breathing, and with the

BELOW: With dear Frank Sinatra and yet another princess, this time Princess Margaret at a swanky function in London.

doctor seemingly not knowing what to do, his grandmother hurriedly grabbed Frank and placed his head under a cold water tap, startling the baby into taking his first gasps of New York air.

In later life, Frank suffered from terrible hearing and ear problems. He maintained it was due to that doctor's negligence, which only fuelled his desire to 'bump into him' even more. As well as being loyal to friends, another of Frank's qualities was that he always bore a deserved grudge.

I didn't meet him again until a decade later, in the mid-60s, at a London restaurant with his then wife Mia Farrow, who was in town making a film called *Guns at Batasi* (in which she replaced Britt Ekland whose new husband Peter Sellers had whisked her to LA for the weekend and refused to allow her back to Pinewood to continue filming) and Frank accompanied her.

'We just love watching *The Saint*,' said Mia, taking me totally unawares.

'We watch it in bed, in our hotel room. It's the best thing on TV,' Frank added.

We had dinner and chatted until the very late hours about movies, TV, London, family and just about everything else. Frank was very grounded and it was clear his success hadn't spoilt him. He also made time to smile and say hello to our fellow diners as they passed our table, which undoubtedly made their night – being in his company certainly made mine.

I can't help think about an old story here probably apocryphal – of a young man who approached Frank in a restaurant, and said, 'Mr Sinatra, I'm so sorry to bother you, but I have my new girlfriend joining me on a dinner-date here this evening, and I wondered if you'd mind saying,

"Hi, Al! How you doing?" when she gets here? It'll really impress her.'

Not wanting to deny the young chap a chance of getting his leg over, Frank said sure, no problem. A couple of minutes later the young lady duly arrived, Al leapt up to greet her and, in walking her to the table, they passed Frank.

'Hey, Al! How you doing, my old friend?' said Frank.

The young man turned around and snapped, 'Oh, fuck off, Frank! Can't you see I'm with my girlfriend?'

I was a huge fan of Frank's, both his music and films, and revelled in his stories over the dinner table. He told me of the making of his movies and the people he'd worked with and hoped to work with in the future. Frank began his musical career in the swing era, with Harry James and Tommy Dorsey – Dorsey in fact called *him* 'kid' as a term of endearment. Frank told me that he realized a large part of their performing success was down to their ability to 'phrase', that is, to 'say play' their instruments and play without appearing to breathe and interrupting the rhythm. Frank took up underwater swimming to help increase his lung capacity and develop his breathing technique. From there, he practised his phrasing method, which you'll see in evidence on screen whenever he sings: he developed a slight twitch in the corner of his mouth through which he breathed in, while expelling air through the rest of his mouth in song.

As well as captivating all audiences with his singing, Frank also had a great screen presence. His ability to glide across it with seeming ease was one I envied greatly. Frank's acting came naturally to him. He was an all-round natural performer, but he only ever did one good take.

George Schlatter, who directed him in several advertisements and TV shows, told me that Frank psyched himself up so much for take one that if you didn't get it on that first shot, then you never would. While he rehearsed dance routines for the big musical numbers, Frank literally walked on to the set word-perfect and ready to go. He never rehearsed dialogue scenes and loathed re-takes.

'Bang-bang-bang, went the scene,' said George. 'And Frank would leave to await the next set-up.' He didn't suffer fools and expected everyone else to be as fully prepared as he was.

I often read about Frank's alleged personal and professional links with Mafia figures such as Sam Giancana, Lucky Luciano and Rocco Fischetti, so I asked him about it.

'Kid, most of the venues I play are, in one way or another, controlled by the Mob – they run Vegas for a start,' he said. 'I turn up at the places and am greeted by all these suited guys who want me to pose for a photo with them. I've no idea who they are, yet in the photos they're standing with their arm around me and appear to be long-lost friends. How many photos have you posed for with people you don't know?'

Mind you, I don't think Frank ever did anything to publicly dispel the rumours of his underworld connections. He rather liked it!

Frank had three children: Nancy Jr, Frank Jr and Tina by his first wife, Nancy Barbato. He was married three more times, to the actresses Ava Gardner, Mia Farrow and finally Barbara Marx, to whom he was married at the time of his death. He, like any loving father, supported his children in every way he could. I remember on Nancy Jr's thirtieth birthday, she opened her present from her father to discover it was a clear $1 million wrapped up. Frank was very generous like that.

When his daughter Tina made the dramatized biography of Frank for TV, apart from miscasting a rather – dare I say – plain-looking actress to play Ava Gardner, she showed her father having a string of affairs – and usually interrupted his bedroom scenes with a phone call to say his wife was in labour! It was a very unflattering biopic to say the least. I broached the subject with his wife, Barbara, and asked what Frank thought of it. She said that she had sat Frank down in the TV room with a large drink and ran the tape for him to watch, alone. When he emerged from the room he said, 'I don't think they quite got me, did they?'

My former wife and I socialized a lot with Frank and Barbara, and spent virtually every Thanksgiving and Easter at their lovely home in Palm Springs, along with Gregory and Veronique Peck, Don Rickles, George and Jolene Schlatter, Cary and Barbara Grant and sometimes the legendary agent Swifty Lazar. They were great days. We would chat, run movies, eat, drink and go swimming in the pool. It was a rare recipe for total relaxation – which Frank relished.

On Easter Sunday Frank would clear us out of the kitchen, and cook his favourite dish of spicy meatballs and pasta. It was the one day on which no one else was allowed to cook. Our only involvement was to help select the accompanying wine.

'Come on down the wine room,' he'd say, 'and choose a bottle.' Frank had one of the best-stocked (and biggest) wine coolers in the world, and was an expert sommelier. After an hour or so of exploring we chose many more than one bottle! Alas, I'm not a great authority on wine, but I can assure you that we drank some pretty good vintages, not to mention expensive ones. But that was Frank – a very generous and attentive host.

One of our other favourite pastimes, aside from drinking copious amounts of Jack Daniels into the night, was gambling. We played the tables in Vegas on many occasions – rarely ever winning much, I might add – and as Frank was very much a night person, he loved it when people stayed up into the early hours with him. It wasn't so much the gambling as the company he loved. He was a very social person and came to life in the late evenings. I couldn't always keep up with him, especially if I needed a clear head the next morning for work.

Frank had a view on hangovers, as he did most things, 'I feel sorry for people who don't drink. When they wake up in the morning, that's as good as they're going to feel all day.'

Despite increasing success, in 1971, at a concert in Hollywood to raise money for the Motion Picture and TV Relief Fund, and at the age of fifty-five, Frank announced that he was retiring. Perhaps he thought he was at the pinnacle of his career, and this was the time to bow out? His self-enforced retirement didn't last long, though – his public wouldn't allow it. Two years later, Frank returned with a television special and an album, both entitled *Ol' Blue Eyes is Back*. He certainly was.

As far as I was concerned, Frank had never changed from the first day I met him. He remained humble, kind, generous and warm. He only ever had praise for me when he saw one of my movies, and when I was cast as James Bond he called to say how delighted he was for me. He never once criticized or offered advice on any of my performances, such as they were, he merely expressed his satisfaction.

Despite various health problems, Frank toured extensively and remained the highest attraction on the worldwide concert circuit during the first half of the 1990s. Alas, at times his memory failed him as did his hearing. I asked how he could still pick up his musical cues. He said he 'felt' it through his feet, via the reverberations on stage. Nothing was going to get in the way of Frank performing.

Having fought bravely against cancer, Frank sadly suffered a heart attack and died at the Cedars–Sinai Medical Center at 10.50 p.m. on 14 May 1998, with wife Barbara and daughter Nancy by his side. His final words were 'I'm losing'.

The following night the lights on the Las Vegas Strip were dimmed. A light had gone out in all our lives. The tributes were manyfold and came from far and wide: Presidents, Prime Ministers, Royalty and, of course, his many friends and fans.

Frank's legacy to the world is a vast one: his many films and TV performances, his many concerts and his many recordings will live on forever, as will my memories of this amazing man who I was so fortunate to be able to call a friend.

⚜

Dean Martin was a former boxer turned comedian, actor, singer and hugely charismatic man. I first encountered him way back in 1952 when, with my then wife, Dorothy Squires, I was in New York and we trotted to Times Square to see 'Dean Martin and Jerry Lewis' at the Paramount Theatre. I'd heard a lot about Dino and Jerry from the cast of the play *Mr Roberts* with whom I'd worked in London – and I was not disappointed. It struck me that,

ABOVE: *The Cannonball Run*, in which I played someone who thought he was Roger Moore.

like Morecambe and Wise in the UK, Dino and Jerry were both very talented individuals in their own right, but together they were dynamite.

A few years later, when I was a contract artist at Warner Bros, I bumped into Dean on the studio lot – where he and Jerry Lewis were making their caper films – several times and exchanged pleasantries.

Later in the decade, of course, he became a founding member of the Rat Pack with Frank Sinatra, Joey Bishop, Sammy Davis Jr and Peter Lawford, and went on to even greater movie success with them in *Ocean's 11*.

With the advent of rock and roll, Dean's career as a crooner was eclipsed by his film work. He was riding high as a movie star and between 1966 and 1969, Dean starred in perhaps his most famous role in four Matt Helm films. They were, in essence, a US version of the Bond movies, though perhaps lighter in style. A planned fifth film, *The Ravagers*, was cancelled after the murder of Dean's co-star and friend Sharon Tate. He said he was too distraught to consider ever playing the character again. In fact, Dean had always been fiercely loyal to his co-stars, as demonstrated when 20th Century Fox fired Marilyn Monroe in *Something's Got to Give* (1962) and then attempted to replace her with Lee Remick. Dean reminded the studio that he had contractual approval of his leading lady and point-blank refused to continue without Monroe. She was re-hired, but sadly died of a drug overdose before shooting could resume. Nine hours of unseen footage remained in the vaults at Fox for decades.

I had to wait until the 1980s before I had the chance to work with Dean in *The Cannonball Run* and he became a very close friend thereafter. I'll never forget when we were shooting in Atlanta, where the cars were all lined up before the race started, and I noticed there were two very pretty showgirls engaged in conversation with Dean. When I sidled over, I smiled and asked, 'Have you just met the new Mrs Martin?' Talk about the eternal flirt!

Contrary to his image as a drinker, Dean told me he'd actually endured a lot of eye surgery in recent years and had been prescribed heavy painkillers, which meant he couldn't drink. In fact he became hooked on the pills for a time. His trademark cigarette and glass in hand was known the world over, but what wasn't known was that the glass was filled with apple juice.

When he toured with Frank and Sammy on the 'Rat Pack Reunion', I occasionally visited and took in a show.

But I noticed Frank (who was first on) would always sing one of Dean's numbers, and then Sammy came on and told one of Dean's gags. So when Dino eventually appeared on stage and the music piped up, Frank would shout, 'We've already sung that!' So Dean would start telling a story …

'I've told that one already!' Sammy would call over. This went on for a few shows and really got under Dean's skin, until one night, as soon as the curtain fell, he took Frank's private plane back alone to LA and refused to ever work with Sinatra again. They only made it up a short time before Dean's death.

I know the greatest tragedy to befall Dean, and one I don't think he ever really recovered from, was when his son, Dean Paul Martin, died in a plane crash in 1987. So much so that, as cancer took hold of my friend in the mid-90s, he consoled his loved ones by saying we shouldn't worry as he'd soon be reunited with his son.

His tombstone carries the title of his most well-known song: 'Everybody Loves Somebody Sometime'.

❧

Sammy Davis Jr was often billed as the 'greatest living entertainer in the world' and no wonder, as son of vaudeville star Sammy Davis Sr, he could do it all: sing, dance, act, perform stand-up comedy, play instruments and do just about anything else you'd care to throw at him.

I was working in television at Warner Bros. when I first met Sammy, and he was a real movie buff who loved nothing better than being around a film studio – whether he was working or not. When I was filming the TV series *Maverick*, he became quite a professional pistol drawer and a past master at gun twirling. I socialized quite a lot with Sammy and realized his fascination with guns hadn't diminished when, in the 1980s, another old pal of mine, lyricist and playwright Leslie Bricusse, threw a dinner party at his home in LA and Sammy arrived, opened his jacket and removed his revolver – handing it to the maid as you would a hat.

Sammy was a hugely funny man and a deeply religious one too. His spirituality stemmed from a near death experience in a car accident in 1954, in San Bernardino, California, as he was making a return trip from Las Vegas to Los Angeles. It was as a result of this accident that he lost his left eye. At the time, it was feared he might lose his other eye, and his friend the actor Jeff Chandler offered one of his own eyes if it would save Sammy from blindness. Thankfully it wasn't needed, but that always struck me as a truly selfless offer. After wearing a patch for a while, Sammy was later fitted with a glass eye, which he wore for the rest of his life.

Though never one to miss an opportunity of sending himself up, Sammy once joked after overhearing someone complaining about discrimination, 'You got it easy! I'm a short, ugly, one-eyed, black Jew. What do you think it's like for me?'

Years later, when he was hosting the Oscars, Sammy remarked, 'Tonight, the Academy honours both my peoples with *Fiddler on the Roof* and *Shaft*.' Audiences around the world loved Sammy's self-deprecating style and wit.

In 1957, Sammy famously became involved with the beautiful Kim Novak, who was then one of Columbia Studios' prized young contract stars. Fearful of any negative press this relationship might attract – and its effect on the studio – boss Harry Cohn called mobster Johnny Roselli and asked him to persuade Sammy to end the affair. Roselli did this by kidnapping Sammy for a few hours and eventually persuading him it was the only way of not having his one good eye ending up on the table. Sammy hastily arranged a marriage to black dancer Loray White for the following year in an attempt to put any controversy to bed, but the union only lasted fifteen months.

I was having dinner with Cubby and Dana Broccoli at the White Elephant in London in the early 1970s and Sammy was at a table across the room. Through a series of gestures he asked if we wanted to go and see a movie with him. Cubby gestured back asking what it was, and Sammy smiled, put a

BELOW: The whole cast on *The Cannonball Run* – including Dean Martin, Sammy Davis Jr, Burt Reynolds and Dom DeLuise – was incredible and the director, Hal Needham, kept several cameras running at all times, just to make sure he didn't miss any of the comedy ad libs.

finger in his mouth and then pointed at the collar line of his neck. None the wiser, we agreed and he then took us to the private cinema at the Mayfair hotel and *Deep Throat* started.

I guess we watched ten or fifteen minutes before Dana suggested we should leave. I think her decision was prompted by the leading lady, having oral sex performed on her, delivering the line: 'Do you mind eating while I smoke?'

Cubby and I grumbled we wouldn't have minded seeing the rest of the film, but our wives did not permit it!

A little while later in Hollywood, Sammy invited us to dinner at his home and he'd had a giant screen installed in his living room to run movies. After dinner, we all settled down and waited for his projector to crank up for the promised 'great movie', and *Behind the Green Door* – the follow-up to *Deep Throat* – started. That was Sammy's sense of humour!

Sammy had been friends with Cubby for years and, in fact, he was offered a part in *Diamonds Are Forever*, which, of course, was filmed in Vegas. Before the sinister assassins Mr Wint and Mr Kidd murder the smuggler Shady Tree, a scene was shot in which Sammy is seen playing roulette at the Whyte House club, and having an exchange with Bert Saxby about contract differences he has with Willard Whyte. The conversation stops when Sammy sees and recognizes James Bond, saying, 'They ain't never gonna get a cake big enough to put him on top of.' Sadly, the scene ended up on the cutting-room floor as it was felt it wasn't needed – and when watching the final running time any 'unnecessary' scenes are the first to go, I'm afraid.

Sammy and Frank Sinatra once (reluctantly) agreed to perform at the MGM Grand hotel in Vegas while sharing the stage with Leo the Lion between them. They were assured it would be safe, as the very old lion would be handled, with a choke chain, by its trainer. In the middle of the number, the beast looked at Sammy and licked its lips, then leaned back on its haunches, as if it was going to leap. Sammy made the sign of the cross. Luckily nothing happened, but after the show Sammy and Frank were having drinks in the lobby and Frank said, 'Boy, I thought that cat was going to come after you there. Hey, Smokey, didn't you turn Jewish? Why did you make the sign of the cross?'

'Well, babe,' Sammy replied, 'I didn't think I would have time to make the Star of David!'

You would often find Sammy in Vegas playing a residency at one of the hotels. Alas, he was a big gambler and, like many entertainers on the strip, he worked there to pay back his losses.

I last saw Sammy a month before he died; he was lying in bed and music legend Quincy Jones was sitting in an armchair next to him. Comatose and full of morphine as he lay dying, Sammy had always been a tiny, thin man but there really wasn't much of him at all that day. The throat cancer that had so tragically struck him had spread. Though when he was told that a laryngectomy would offer him the best chance of survival, Sammy replied he would rather keep his voice and face the illness than have a part of his throat removed.

After his death, Frank Sinatra paid off many of Sammy's outstanding debts.

CHAPTER 7

The Creative Geniuses

I T'S TRUE TO SAY THAT BEHIND EVERY GOOD ACTOR STANDS A terrific writer and a highly talented director. Bryan Forbes, or Brownie as I always called him, and I first met during our National Service sixty-odd years ago, when we were both stationed with the Combined Services Entertainment Unit in Hamburg. We became great friends, and I'm happy to say that that extended into a very happy working relationship when Bryan was head of ABPC films and, in 1970, green-lit what I have always believed is my best film, *The Man Who Haunted Himself.* He later directed me in *Sunday Lovers* and, when Cannon Films approached me to make a film for them in 1985 and I suggested the Sidney Sheldon book *The Naked Face,* they asked if I had a director in mind – without hesitation I told them to call Bryan.

Bryan's stories of his adventures in the film business were wonderful. For example, there was the time in the late 1950s when Cubby Broccoli came to England with Alan Ladd Jr to make *The Black Knight.* It was not a promising script, but

LEFT: With Bryan Forbes and his wife, Nanette Newman, in St Mark's Square, Venice.

Bryan Forbes green-lit *The Man Who Haunted Himself* (ABOVE), which I consider to be my best film (seen here with Hildegarde Neil); and directed *Sunday Lovers* (seen here with Lynn Redgrave and Priscilla Barnes). The tagline on the poster for *Sunday Lovers* was 'NEVER has turned to ALWAYS on a Sunday'. Fun to make? Yes, I think that's a fair assumption …

a cast including Peter Cushing, Patricia Medina and some of the best technicians alive was assembled.

Bryan was drafted in to work on the script as, early on in his writing career, he was a contract script doctor, called in to perform emergency surgery on terminal cases. Bryan described *The Black Knight* as 'the brainchild of half a dozen parents'.

One Saturday afternoon the producers rang him to say that they had reached an impasse. 'We've run out of pages,' they told him. 'Could you come up with something by Monday morning?'

Bryan was young and hungry, and with the misguided confidence that often goes with these two factors, he agreed and was shown footage of what had already been shot and what needed to be bridged.

The one big problem, he discovered, was that Sue Ladd – Alan's wife – had script approval. Sue, who had been an actress herself and was Ladd's agent, was quite a force to be reckoned with, and every word uttered by Ladd had to first be approved by her. Bryan came up with a few pages in which Ladd dodged arrows, vaulted from the castle battlements into a cart of hay, sliced a few of the villains in two with his sword, seized a horse and galloped across the rising drawbridge just in time.

What was Mrs Ladd's verdict?

'Alan Ladd does not steal horses.'

She went on to explain that if he did, they would lose the Boy Scouts Association, the Daughters of the American Revolution and probably half his fan club. Everyone was dumbfounded. However, Cubby's partner, Irving Allen said, 'Sue, he's not *stealing* a horse, he's *borrowing* one.'

She was not convinced. So Bryan came up with a

solution. After Ladd had done all his vaulting and slicing he strode towards a sentry and uttered the immortal words: 'Is this the horse I ordered?' He then jumps onto it and gallops off. Sue agreed it! And that's what they shot.

You quite honestly could not make these stories up! It's almost as bad as dear Tony Curtis saying: 'Yonder lies da castle of my foddah,' in (reportedly) *The Black Shield of Falworth*.

As much fun as that sounds, dear reader, it is a somewhat apocryphal story perpetuated by Debbie Reynolds. Tony actually delivered the line: 'Yonder in the valley of the sun is my father's castle' in a film called *Son of Ali Baba*. Debbie, in a TV interview, misquoted it (and the film) and somehow the story stuck in the minds of the public.

Years later, Tony was at Hugh Hefner's house at a party and Hef greeted him with, 'Yonder likes da castle of my foddah.'

'I never said that,' Tony replied coolly.

'Then don't tell anybody,' Hef said. 'It makes a great movie story!'

Bryan was never averse to sharing his movie stories with a wider audience, and many years ago he volunteered as a prison visitor to do just that. One time, he gave a lecture of some pith and moment (or so he believed) about the film industry and then asked for questions. A hand went up immediately: 'Is Lana Turner a good fuck?'

Bryan saw then that his erudition had fallen on stony ground!

❧

Tom Mankiewicz, who had written a couple of my Bond

scripts, was the son of Joseph L. Mankiewicz, who wrote and directed *Cleopatra*, and consequently he had many a tale to regale us with on set. One of my favourites was how, in 1961, young Tom landed himself the job of production assistant on *The Comancheros*, a Western starring John Wayne, Stuart Whitman and Lee Marvin. It was directed by the renowned Hungarian director Michael Curtiz, though John Wayne also took a co-director credit.

They were on location in Moab, Utah and were setting up a scene where 200 head of cattle were being driven towards a canyon. Seeing the twenty-foot sheer drop ahead of them, Mankiewicz asked Curtiz what would happen to the cattle.

'They'll go over the edge. Those that die we'll sell for carpets,' he was told.

'You can't kill the poor animals!' exclaimed Tom, amazed at the director's total lack of regard for life.

'You're fired!' snapped Curtiz. 'Get off my set!'

Tom headed back to his motel and had started packing when the phone rang. It was 'Duke' Wayne.

'What are you doing, kid?' he asked.

'I'm packing, Mr Wayne. I've been fired.'

'Were you the kid who saved my cattle?'

'Your cattle, sir?'

'Yes, my cattle!' said Wayne. 'Start unpacking again and get back to the set — you're now my assistant.'

The next day the production team were setting up a sequence in which the Indians charge over the hill towards the heroes. Back then, there were no such luxuries as walkie-talkies or mobile phones and as the cameras were set way back from the hill in order to capture the full panoramic widescreen shot, the director decided he needed someone up there to signal the Indians when to charge.

'Can anyone ride a pony?' he asked.

Being gung-ho, Tom stepped forward. 'Yes, sir, I can.'

The next thing he knew, Tom was in the make-up chair being blacked-up and, wearing a loincloth and with a full headdress of feathers, headed up to the brow of the distant hill on his mount. There he waited, watching for a white handkerchief being waved by the assistant – his signal to lead the charge downhill. All went swimmingly and Tom came galloping down towards the camera and, now fully into his character, as he drew near to the camera, threw himself off and at one of our cowboy heroes.

After the director called 'Cut!', Wayne sidled up to Tom.

'Was that you on that pony, kid?'

'Yes, sir!' said Tom, proudly.

'Kid, you looked like a monkey fucking a football!' The Duke offered as he walked away smiling.

Tom wisely gave up stunt work and moved into screenwriting and directing thereafter.

⚜

I suppose the one downside to reaching eighty-six years of age is that I'm now losing a lot of my mates. Sadly, in January 2013, Michael Winner joined the cutting-room staff upstairs. (When we were filming *The Persuaders!*, whenever we heard the news of an actor or director dying, Tony Curtis would say, 'That's another one gone to the great cutting-room in the sky!') Despite being friends forever, I only made one film with Michael – called *Bullseye!* – in which Michael Caine starred with me (or did I star with him?). The film wasn't … how can I put this … it

ABOVE: Say what you like about *Bullseye!* but working with Michael Caine and Michael Winner was always a joy.

wasn't the highlight of either of our careers (or Michael Winner's come to that). In fact, one day Michael Caine leaned across to me and said, "Ere, Rog, this film is going to be our bleeding *Ishtar*," likening the experience to the film that was at that point the biggest flop in the history of Columbia Pictures.

Mr Winner was certainly one of the more animated directors I worked with and one who liked to be heard on set. In fact, that reminds me of a story I heard about when he was shooting his first film at Pinewood in the early 1960s, called *Play It Cool*.

Michael decided he'd like to use a megaphone on set, and called out all of his instructions through it. The poor

MICHAEL
CAINE

PREVIOUS PAGES: I've known Michael Caine for over fifty years now. Not a lot of people know that.

cameraman, who was sitting about three feet away from the director, even had his orders barked through the loudhailer. It got to a point where, during a short break, the cameraman in question excused himself from set and disappeared down the corridor. Ten minutes later, and ready to continue, Mr Winner was furious to see the camera devoid of an operator, and screamed, 'Where is he?'

'Gone to the toilet,' replied some helpful spark.

With that, dear Michael marched down the corridor, flung open the lavatory door and saw that the middle cubicle was occupied. 'Are you in there?' he shouted.

'Yes,' came the reply. 'But, Michael, please go away. I can only deal with one shit at a time!'

As well as directing, Michael often produced, wrote, cast and edited his films, though usually under the pseudonym Arnold Crust. Many of the credits for photographs that later appeared in his newspaper column were also credited to Arnold Crust or Arnold Crust Jr. Being modest, Michael didn't want to take all the credit himself.

On set, we noticed Winner would develop a small red blush on each cheek which, as it grew larger, gave us prior warning of him about to explode. It was a nuance we used to our advantage as whenever Michael Caine and I saw his cheeks reddening we'd say, 'Here it comes!' and warn any new actor on set, just as our beloved director gave 'what for' to some poor unsuspecting person. Never before had I known a director who would fire people instantly on set, though once the shouting was over, Winner would turn to us and say, 'Oh, how lovely! We've got rid of him. Right, let's continue, dears!'

I have to say, his bark was far worse than his bite, and he really was a very kind and caring man. When a rather famous production secretary confided in him that she was about to undergo treatment for cancer and would be unable to start his next film, he immediately arranged for her to go private, and in the best hospital too.

Sadly, Michael had been ill, and in and out of hospital himself, ever since consuming a bad oyster in 2007. He told me, on numerous occasions, of how he underwent scores of operations, dying several times on the table, but each time he bounced back and defied the doctors' pessimistic prognosis.

In the summer of 2012 he was told he had only two years left to live, and even joked about it in his newspaper column. Such was his spirit that, even from his hospital bed and throughout his long illness, he continued to write his *Sunday Times* restaurant reviews – only he had the restaurants send the food in to him.

Michael had written his restaurant reviews 'Winner's Dinners' in the *Sunday Times* since 1994, and he used to mail me photocopies of the column when I was abroad. Aside from being a critic, he was also a great host at any meal. Our last memorable dinner together was after his final 'Winner's Dinners Awards', which was held at the Belvedere Restaurant (chosen because of its close proximity to his house in Kensington), and afterwards Michael and his long-term partner Geraldine invited us back to their home for a superb dinner. At the table were Knights of the Realm Michael Parkinson, David Frost, Tim Rice and me, together with Lord Lloyd Webber and our respective wives.

It was a hysterically funny dinner, with Michael being the host par excellence, despite his occasional good-humoured screams to the kitchen for the next course.

Although famous for having many girlfriends, there was one in particular who remained very dear to Michael. He'd known Geraldine since 1957, and they got together again in the early 2000s. Geraldine was at Michael's side every day he spent in hospital and helped nurse him back to health. Such was his love for Geraldine that after returning home he proposed to her and threw a big engagement party at the Ritz where he warned everyone, 'It's taken me this long to get engaged, so don't expect a wedding anytime soon.'

Over three years later, Mr Winner was enjoying all the benefits of wedded life but hadn't actually made the commitment of marrying Geraldine. One evening at Scott's restaurant in Mayfair, Kristina and I joined Michael and Geraldine, the Caines and the Bricusses and turned the conversation around to marriage. We told him he'd been engaged long enough and his reasons for remaining a bachelor were no longer convincing. We all urged him to make the commitment. The wedding followed in 2011 and I know it made Michael the happiest man on earth.

Aside from films, his other great passion was the Police Memorial Trust, a charity dedicated to raising plinths in memory of policemen and women killed in the line of duty. In 2005 he presided as the Queen unveiled the National Police Memorial in The Mall, designed by Norman Foster. Ever the film director, Michael called Her Majesty 'dear' when she unveiled the memorial.

Michael was offered an OBE for his work on behalf of the police, but turned it down remarking, 'an OBE is what you get if you clean the toilets well at King's Cross Station'.

My last conversation with him was towards the end of 2012, when I called to wish him a happy birthday. He'd just returned from another stay in intensive care and sounded terribly weak. Sadly, his liver was in failing health and a short time afterwards, Michael called 'Cut' on his final scene. As per the Jewish faith, his funeral took place within a couple of days of his passing and, sadly, I wasn't able to be there.

Fittingly, his memorial on 23 June 2013 was held at his beloved National Police Memorial and I was delighted to attend with Kristina and speak, along with Michael Caine, Michael Parkinson, Leslie Bricusse and a whole roster of police nobility, all keen to express their gratitude to Michael for establishing permanent memorials to their fallen colleagues.

BELOW: Celebrating Michael Winner's seventieth birthday. He chartered a private plane and flew us all to Venice. (*back row, l to r*) Leslie Bricusse, Terry O'Neill, Johnny Gold, me, Michael Caine, and (*front row*) Andrew Lloyd Webber and Michael Winner.

He was a great director, a talented writer and tireless charity worker, but more than that he was a real character who enjoyed nothing more than taking the rise out of himself with his newspaper columns, letters pages and in person.

One story I wish I'd told Michael related to my assistant Gareth, who does a rather good impersonation of the great man. On occasion Gareth would call up our travel agent, driver and airport VIP service lady (who had all dealt with Michael Winner over the years, and had the scars to prove it), along with other unsuspecting innocents and would bark down the telephone at them with the most bizarre requests.

That was all well and good until a driver we used to use called Gareth in a fit of hysterics. It was fast approaching Christmas, and thus a busy time for car companies, so when Eddie took a call from 'Michael Winner', who was ranting on about wanting four cars that evening and how he dare not be late and so on, Eddie said, 'Fuck off, Gareth. I haven't got time for this today!' and hung up.

A few seconds later the phone rang again and the voice said, 'Eddie Wilcox, this is Michael Winner! Did you just hang up on me?'

'Oh! Hello, erm, Michael,' said a sheepish Eddie, 'I'm sorry, I think we had a crossed line there!'

'OK, dear,' said the great man. 'Now, about cars for my staff Christmas outing ...'

He'd have laughed so much had he known about Gareth's mischief. I really don't think we'll ever see his like again.

Another great pal who is mentioned many times within these pages is composer and lyricist Leslie Bricusse, and that's because Leslie's always been around throughout my life. It was when I moved to Stanmore during my days on *The Saint* that I first met Leslie, at a restaurant called Maxim's. We hit it off immediately and a friendship developed. Mind you, soon after that I worked with Leslie's wife, Yvonne Romain (Evie), on an episode of *The Saint* entitled 'The King of the Beggars', in which we both dressed down to play down-and-outs – so I know I was destined to get to know the lovely couple, one way or another.

As well as being a talented lyricist and composer with hit musicals *Stop the World – I Want to Get Off*, *Pickwick* and *Doctor Dolittle* to his credit, Leslie is also an accomplished playwright and I've collaborated with him on two projects, *Sunday Lovers* and *Bullseye!*, one of which I'm sure he'd probably rather forget – I'll leave you to guess which.

We would often meet up for dinner with Jackie Collins and Oscar Lerman and Johnny and Jan Gold, along with Leslie and Evie at their house in Beverly Hills. Even when they weren't at home, I quite often stayed at the house when I had to go to Hollywood.

Evie and Leslie also had homes in Acapulco and Portofino at various times, and I stayed in those, too. In fact, I distinctly remember being at the Italian house when Neil Armstrong took the first step on the moon, as Leslie woke me up to watch it on TV.

It was on that trip that he told me he was building a home in St Paul in the South of France, and, then living by the water in Tuscany myself, I couldn't understand why someone would want to build up in the hills, miles from anywhere and a half-hour drive from the ocean. It was only

ABOVE: With Yvonne – Evie – Romain in an episode of *The Saint* called 'The King of the Beggars' back in the 1960s. Yes, that's me on the left, raising an eyebrow.

when I visited that house – and I'm actually very grateful to Leslie for the free holidays I've had – that I fell in love with the area and knew *exactly* why he wanted to build there. On one occasion when I had to be out of England for a while, for tax reasons, Leslie was having some work done at the house in St Paul and asked me to move in and supervise the builders. A fair exchange, I reckoned.

It was at that time I discovered, via local architect Robert Dallas, a plot of land on which foundations for a house had been laid was lying abandoned, with the developer having run out of money. I put in a bid, and that is how I came to own my pad in St Paul.

At St Paul, we have the best restaurant you could want right on our doorstep – the Colombe d'Or. Kristina and I still take our holidays there and in the five decades I've been visiting I don't think it's changed much at all. Whenever I come into the tree-lined courtyard, I think back to seeing regular visitors Simone Signoret and Yves Montand sitting in the corner, in their favourite spot. They loved it so much that they were married there, too. I had lunch with Yves in the mid-80s, a while after Simone passed away, and he explained that he'd met a lady who had fallen pregnant.

'I think I've made a mistake, Roger,' he said, 'and the child will grow up without knowing his father.' Yves died just three years later, aged seventy, on the set of *IP5: The Island of Pachyderms*. It was the very last day of shooting and, after his very last shot, he literally dropped dead of a heart attack.

Although I no longer live in St Paul, my connection with the village continues as my son Christian was married there, and since my last book there have been additions to the Moore ranks as Christian and his wife, Lara, are now the proud parents of Tristan, who was born in December

2009, and Maximillian who was born in November 2011. Both boys were baptised in the same church in which their parents were married.

It was also through Leslie Bricusse that I met Danny Kaye. Of course, I knew of him, and had seen many of his shows, but through getting to know him I came to appreciate how magical Danny was, not only as an entertainer but as a humanitarian as well. He had a natural ability to make children smile, quite often children who had little to smile about. Danny became the first UNICEF Goodwill Ambassador and I'm so grateful to be able to help continue, in my own modest way, the work he started.

After Danny's death, his daughter Dena invited me and the Bricusses to join her for one last meal in the kitchen Danny loved (and the room where we'd enjoyed so many marvellous meals – he was a terrific chef) before the house was sold. The only thing missing was Danny rushing into another room afterwards to watch a VHS show of himself conducting an orchestra – he loved to conduct, and loved sharing the experience with friends, although I don't think he'd ever read music, he just felt the rhythm.

Director Roy Baker, with whom I'd happily worked on many episodes of *The Saint*, had himself earlier worked with Alfred Hitchcock as an assistant director at Gainsborough Studios. Roy maintained he learned a tremendous amount from Hitch, chief amongst which was that 'time spent on preparation was seldom ever wasted'. However, Hitch didn't have a great love of actors, once famously describing them as 'cattle'. When Roy was assisting him, one hapless actress appeared on set for her first day of shooting, and after the first take Hitch looked up and said, 'Cut! I wind her up, I put her down but she don't go! Bring me *Spotlight!*' (the actors' directory). He could be a very cruel man at times.

Hitchcock reserved a particular dislike for those thespians who employed the 'method' technique. When directing Ingrid Bergman, the star turned and said, 'Hitch, what is my motivation for this scene?'

In front of the entire crew Hitchcock snapped back, 'It's only a bloody film, Ingrid!'

It reminded me of a story I heard about Laurence Olivier and Dustin Hoffman working together on *The Marathon Man* – and you'll never feel the same about visiting the dentist again. One of the scenes between the duo took place just as Dustin's character arrived the worse for having been out running. Being a keen advocate of 'the method' Dustin actually went on a sprint around the studio grounds before reporting on set, and was genuinely out of breath, ready for the call of 'Action'. A rather concerned Olivier leaned across to him and said, 'Have you ever thought about just acting out of breath, dear boy?'

One of Roy Baker's more unusual films for Rank starred Dirk Bogarde and John Mills and featured veiled intimations of homosexuality in New Mexico – and it always really intrigued me as to why any of them made it.

After the success of two 1950s films for Rank – *The One That Got Away* and *A Night to Remember* – Roy signed a three-picture contract with the company, and Pinewood's head of production, Earl St John, handed him a book called *The Singer Not the Song*.

'I thought it was awful, and I told him so,' Roy later told me. 'I came to the table with three other projects which were, one by one, rejected. Earl said that he really wanted me to do *The Singer Not the Song* with Dirk Bogarde.'

Bogarde was then Rank's highest-paid artist and, nearing the end of his seven-year contract, was keen to get away from the pretty boy heroes he'd largely played for the studio; though he'd made it clear he didn't really want to do *this* film.

Catapulted into this strange scenario, Roy dutifully flew out to LA to see Dirk Bogarde and discuss the picture but he soon discovered that for some reason Bogarde was angry about Johnny Mills being cast to star opposite him. Mills, on the other hand, had a different take on the project and said when he was first offered the film, he was to co-star with Marlon Brando. Naturally, he was very excited, but for some reason Brando pulled out and that's when Dirk came in. All this caused a great deal of tension on the set but Roy soldiered on through it and made it look as good as possible. However, as good as it looked, they finished up with a picture that was panned by everyone.

The last film notwithstanding, Roy had enjoyed great success in the UK and later went to Hollywood, where he famously directed Marilyn Monroe in *Don't Bother to Knock*. The experience, however, was not a particularly happy one, as he later discovered that Joseph Schenck, one of the production chiefs at 20th Century Fox, had decided to green-light the film as an indulgence to Marilyn, despite her being terribly miscast in the role (Roy suggested Jane Wyman should have played the part by the way). The studio head, Darryl Zanuck, thought it was all a waste of time but as Monroe was under contract they were obliged to find her a film, and with nothing else on offer he let it go ahead, on the proviso that it was made as cheaply as possible.

Marilyn, meanwhile, demonstrating her great insecurity, was adamant she'd only work if her dialogue coach, Natasha Lytess, was on set at all times. Zanuck point-blank refused, and wrote to Marilyn, saying she had 'built up a Svengali and if you are going to progress with your career and become as important talent-wise as you have publicity-wise then you must destroy this Svengali before it destroys you. When I cast you for the role I cast you as an individual.'

Nevertheless, on day one Miss Lytess appeared on set and sat down next to the camera.

Roy had terrible problems with Marilyn's timekeeping as she'd often arrive two or three hours after everyone else was ready and on set. Such was her insecurity that despite countless rehearsals she never quite knew when to pick up a cue or how to move across set; every take would be different. She'd seek constant reassurance from her Svengali and thought more about how she should *act* rather than just naturally being the character.

Eventually, with schedules overrunning, Miss Lytess was barred from the set and Roy said that when he told Marilyn he had expected her to react badly, but she quietly accepted the situation. In fact, she later admitted to being so confused that she'd let anyone be her friend and advise her – though it went to extremes when she let her dialogue coach pass judgement on everything she said and did in her professional life and in private too.

Roy offered Marilyn every reassurance she needed on set and finished the movie on schedule, quite possibly drawing out one of Marilyn's best, if underrated, performances.

I never met Miss Monroe myself, but my hairdresser on *Ivanhoe* – a lovely, if somewhat camp, chap named Gordon Bond – used to tell me stories of working with her, usually when I was in the make-up chair, where he'd make a habit of pressing his manhood against my shoulder while telling me stories about his Spanish boyfriend and saying things like, 'My matador is coming home for the weekend.'

Anyhow, Gordon had worked on *The Prince and the Showgirl* at Pinewood with Laurence Olivier and Marilyn Monroe, and said he had terrible problems (as did everyone) with Marilyn's terrible timekeeping. But alas – poor Gordon! – when he had spent an hour or two preparing her hair for the shoot, Arthur Miller would come into the dressing room, squeeze Marilyn's shoulder and take her into the room next door … from which they'd emerge thirty minutes later and Gordon would have to do her hair all over again.

One day on a location shoot, Gordon hitched a ride in Marilyn's car. The scene involved the Marines and Queen's Guards, who'd been drafted in, and as the Prince (as played by Olivier) arrived, they were to give him the full military welcome.

Marilyn got out of her car and, as Gordon stepped out behind her, half the guards, who'd dutifully ignored her, called out, 'Oh! Hello, Gordon!'

While working at Fox, Roy Baker said one of the production executives was a chap named Sol Wurtzel. Actually, the whole Wurtzel family were employed at the studio in one capacity or another, be it in the carpenter's shop, the transport department – and everywhere else. One young starlet who was signed to the ranks was advised that her career might progress if she 'stepped out' with Mr Wurtzel. Keen to advance, she willingly did so but after a few months realized she was getting nowhere and only then discovered she'd been going out with the wrong Mr Wurtzel – her guy worked in the paint shop. Only in Hollywood!

⁂

I couldn't write about Hollywood and not mention my dear friend Albert Romolo Broccoli, also known as Cubby, who was one of its biggest and most successful film producers. He was born in April 1909 in a tenement block in Astoria, Queens, New York, but almost didn't survive, as his was a breech birth and he had trouble breathing. His grandmother Marietta, who had emigrated from Calabria to America in 1897, resorted to a traditional remedy – the insertion of the head of a black chicken into the child's mouth. The treatment worked and the boy started to breathe again. Thank goodness for all of us!

Cubby didn't enjoy a financially rich childhood, far from it. But in 1934, with the encouragement of his cousin Pat de Cicco, who had left his family farming business to become a Hollywood agent, Cubby travelled to LA to break into show business.

At first, life was tough and Cubby sold hair products and Christmas trees to get by. However, his cousin was a successful agent and was well placed to introduce him to people such as the actor Cary Grant, with whom Cubby became great friends, director Howard Hughes, who employed him as an assistant on the film *The Outlaw*, and Charles Feldman, who gave him a job at his talent agency. Cubby then made the transition from agent to film producer, working with partner Irving Allen.

Having established himself in the LA film industry, Cubby first travelled to Britain in 1948, where he cut an

ABOVE: Dear Cubby Broccoli was a great friend to me – and fearless too (although the tiger is stuffed, I think).

incongruous figure in our austerity-shrouded post-World War II capital.

'Where's the King's Arms?' he once asked a local.

'Around the Queen's arse!' he was told – a sardonic reply that delighted him. He still laughed about that years later.

Cubby booked into the Savoy on that first trip, and went into the Grill to have breakfast. A waiter came to the table and asked, 'What would you like, sir?'

'I'll have bacon and eggs and a pot of coffee,' came the reply.

The waiter had to explain that, due to rationing, that wouldn't be possible. However, a couple of days later, the same waiter turned up at Cubby's breakfast table saying he had a surprise. Underneath a big silver lid, he unveiled two boiled eggs. Cubby asked the waiter how he had got them. 'I brought them from home,' he said.

Cubby was so touched that he immediately became a champion of all things British, and every movie he made thereafter was in Britain. He loved the lifestyle: the horse racing, the gambling clubs (where I first met him) and the social scene.

His first film as a producer, and one he made in London, was *The Red Beret*. He and his producing partner, Irving Allen, decided Alan Ladd would be the perfect star and Cubby was despatched to meet with the actor. Cubby told me he had thought it was odd that Irving Allen didn't want to accompany him to the meeting, though he later discovered why. Alan Ladd, who started out in the business as a camera grip technician in the late 1930s, had worked on a series that Irving Allen directed and had mentioned his aspirations to become an actor.

'Why do you want to be an out-of-work actor?' Allen

asked him. 'Stay as a grip, you'll make more money.'

Well, by the early 1950s Ladd had indeed become an actor – one of Hollywood's most popular – and was earning $100,000 a year under contract. By 1952, however, he felt he was worth more and asked for a raise. It was not forthcoming, so he refused to renew his contract.

Cubby told me that at the time he didn't even have enough money to pay his rent that month but the prospect of *The Red Beret* being green-lit if he could secure Hollywood's biggest actor was too great an opportunity to miss, so he took a gamble and told Ladd's agent, Lew Wasserman, that they could pay $200,000 for this one film, plus ten per cent of the profits.

Wasserman turned Cubby down, saying he was just starting out and was 'an amateur'.

Realizing Ladd's wife, Sue, actually called the shots in that camp, and having heard that she fancied a trip to Europe, Cubby called her to explain his $200,000 offer had been rejected.

'Stay by the phone,' Sue snapped.

A few minutes later she called back, inviting Cubby to meet her later that day. Also at the meeting was a rather pale-faced Lew Wasserman, who'd obviously felt the wrath of Sue Ladd. She told him to go ahead and make the deal, but Lew told her that he felt it was crazy.

'You haven't got Alan any more than this!' she barked at him.

The deal was done, and in fact became the first of three pictures the producers made with Ladd, thus launching Cubby's career as a mainstream film producer. That first film, incidentally, was directed by Terence Young, and written by Richard Maibaum – both of whom, of course, went on to collaborate on the early Bond films.

ABOVE: At the opening of the second 007 stage at Pinewood with (*l to r*) Fiona Fullerton, Cubby Broccoli, Tanya Roberts, Christopher Walken and Alison Doody.

I feel I should also mention the important role a young female writer named Johanna Harwood made to the early days of the Bond series too, because her involvement has often been overlooked and her pivotal role clouded by the vagaries of film history and the egos of those within. Johanna is actually a neighbour of mine in Monaco, though she's long since hung up her typewriter ribbon.

Having started in film continuity in her native Ireland,

Johanna became 'assistant continuity' on *The Red Beret*, but her involvement in Bond came not via Cubby, but Harry Saltzman. With a shortage of film work, Johanna had taken employment with a theatrical agency in London, but it was soon taken over by Harry Saltzman and she became his secretary and script reader. Her talent for writing developed and she authored many articles and stories, including a James Bond magazine spoof in 1959, and so when Harry had an idea for a film one day he asked Johanna to write an outline for him. Johanna was subsequently handed books Harry had read and felt could be film subjects.

'I had to write film outlines or first draft scripts,' she told me, 'so that Harry could tout them around financiers in the hope of raising funds. When he optioned Ian Fleming's books, and was trying to create interest in making a film, I adapted *Dr No* for him. It was a first draft script.'

When Harry and Cubby came together to found EON Productions, they initially intended to film *Thunderball* but legal issues surrounding the book prompted Harry to pull out Harwood's *Dr No* script.

'Terence Young was a terrible misogynist,' Johanna told me, 'and so the idea of working with a female scriptwriter didn't appeal one bit. He brought in Wolf Mankowitz, who wanted to make the villain a monkey – which appalled Cubby – and then Richard Maibaum and Berkely Mather (whose novel *The Pass Beyond Kashmir* had been optioned by the duo that year) were brought in to add a man's touch. However, it was largely my script they ended up filming, as it was closest to Fleming's book.'

During filming of *Dr No*, Johanna was dispatched to Paris to start work on adapting another of Fleming's books, *From Russia with Love*. Consequently she only ever visited the set of *Dr No* once for a meeting with the producers. She later heard Terence Young dismiss her as 'my script girl', suggesting she only contributed one or two ideas in the screenplay.

Though she later wrote the screenplay for *Call Me Bwana*, which EON produced in 1962, she moved to Paris to work for Reader's Digest, having grown somewhat dispirited by the (then) male-dominated industry.

Bwana, incidentally, was all set in Africa but the crew didn't get quite that far. Gerrard's Cross Golf Club, a mile or so from Pinewood Studios, doubled for the location, with the addition of plastic palm trees and three imported giraffes, an elephant and a zebra. At night they used to let the animals roam around the course – simply closing the gate at the end of the day's shoot. Filmed in the freezing winter, back at the studio they would knock the snow off the potted palms and pretend it was Africa. The fact you can see the actors' breath in the film didn't matter – much like in my days shooting the glamorous locations of *The Saint* on the Elstree backlot.

Aside from *Bwana,* and *Chitty Chitty Bang Bang* in 1968, Cubby concentrated primarily on producing Bond films for the rest of his life. When once asked if he felt frustrated at having confined himself to 007, he said that he had a tiger by the tail and that he couldn't let it go!

It's incredible to think that we are all now looking forward to the twenty-fourth Bond film – twenty-four films and *still* the world's biggest film franchise! I can't wait, personally. I think Daniel Craig is a tremendous Bond and I know that Cubby would have been delighted to see him in the role – he's the perfect 007 and looks as though he could actually kill ... whereas I just hugged or bored them to death ...

CHAPTER 8

The Producers

While the writers and directors come up with interesting ways to spend the money, it's the producer's job to raise it. Apart from being perhaps the most prolific of all British film producers, Harry Alan Towers was one of the more colourful characters of the British film business, racking up over 100 big-screen producing credits, plus another fifty-odd as a writer. Granted, many of them were cheaply made action, horror and soft-porn movies, but Harry had no interest in winning plaudits or awards; he just wanted to entertain and make a quick profit.

Though I never worked with him, I knew many cast and crew who did and who, in turn, regaled me with their tales.

One such was from Fred Turner, who was the managing director of Rank Film Distributors in the 1980s and 1990s. When Fred took his annual holiday one year, Harry – or El Sombrero as he was known by his crews due to his initials

LEFT: Producer Elliott Kastner – with whom I'd worked on *North Sea Hijack* in the late 1970s – used every trick in the book to make sure he got the film he wanted. Nothing wrong with that – it's what all good producers do.

HAT – rolled up to see Fred's deputy and said, 'George, I've got this most wonderful script by a very talented writer named Peter Welbeck and I think it's right up your street.'

Harry didn't bank on the Deputy MD knowing that Peter Welbeck was in fact his pseudonym and the script had been knocking around Wardour Street for months. That was Harry, always looking for the main chance.

Peter Manley, who was production manager on some of my *Saints* and made a few films with El Sombrero, told me about one time he was with Harry on a film in Marrakesh. Apparently every weekend HAT would go off to London with the negative in his suitcase and the following Monday he would arrive back with a case full of unexposed film and cash to pay the crew – all highly illegal back then, of course.

One Monday Harry didn't come back – and by Wednesday there was still no sign of him and the crew were about to mutiny and stop shooting. Peter persuaded them to carry on, as he knew they would be in a better bargaining position if they were still working.

Sure enough, the following week Harry arrived and asked how it was all going, but he hadn't brought any cash with him. It wasn't untypical of Harry to have cash-flow problems. He asked for the film that had been shot in his absence but – thinking on his feet – Peter told him it was in the hotel safe and couldn't be released until Harry had paid the crew. Harry fumed and jumped up and down a bit but then shot off somewhere, only to return a day later with the cash.

Harry was a chancer, a charmer and a shrewd businessman who would put together the most obscure and complicated co-production deals involving countries you'd never heard of, and he found film-friendly tax shelters in the furthest-

ABOVE: Sir Larry Olivier and producer Harry Alan Towers – HAT or El Sombrero to his friends – another producer who knew a few tricks.

flung corners of the world. He churned his movies out at a rate of knots – mainly because he had to make the next film to pay off his debts and crews on the last.

He would never *not* pay, he was just very tardy.

John Llewellyn Moxey, who directed some of my *Saints*, made one picture for Towers but 'stopped shooting until my cheque cleared', he said.

Director Michael Tuchner checked into a hotel somewhere in deepest Europe one day while on a recce for a (non-HAT) production. The manager greeted him warmly and said, 'I understand you are in the film business?'

'Yes, that's right,' said Michael.

'Do you know Mr Harry Alan Towers?'

'Well, I know *of* him,' Tuchner replied.

'Then please would you take this bill to London and ask him to settle it?' asked the distraught manager.

HAT would often shoot two films back to back or in the same locale to benefit from the economies of scale. One such case was when *The Call of the Wild* was on location a few miles from his big-screen version of *Treasure Island* with Orson Welles, supposedly one of his oldest friends. Peter Manley, who was associate producer on *The Call of the Wild*, suggested to HAT that it would be great to have Orson Welles appear in his film in a day role, and might he consider allowing Welles to come over from the other side of the valley? Realizing that Orson would ask for more money, Towers declined, saying, 'I wouldn't wish him on you, Peter!'

Incidentally, of the former film, its star, Charlton Heston, said, 'The worst film I ever made was *The Call of the Wild*. How can you possibly screw up that story? You may well ask. The root of our troubles was the producer, a sort of rogue Brit who flickered shadowlike in and out of the country to avoid his various creditors. What we finally ended up with was a joint British/American/Norwegian/ German/French/Italian/Spanish co-production. There are many good actors in all these countries whose English is perfectly competent. Our producer did not hire them.' Ouch.

For many years HAT could not enter the US without the threat of being arrested, after jumping bail there in 1961. By all accounts he would arrive in New York with some lovely ladies and, to help seal various finance deals for his films, he would leave the young ladies with the executives for the afternoon … and very obliging they were too, I hear. The vice ring was soon uncovered and Towers was arrested.

HAT made a living from adapting public domain stories and was not averse to a little thinly disguised plagiarism. He would often arrive on location for one film, having written a screenplay for the next film on the plane over. Yet, despite his sausage factory approach, Towers managed to attract big-name actors such as Orson Welles, Jack Palance, Michael Caine and Christopher Lee – sometimes more than once. In fact, my *Golden Gun* adversary starred in five of HAT's *Fu Manchu* films, based on the characters created by Sax Rohmer. The first, *The Face of Fu Manchu,* was rather good but then …

'*Brides of Fu Manchu* was tosh,' Christopher said. 'An extravagant publicity stunt almost sank the picture. At the instigation of producer Harry Alan Towers, who took an enthusiastic part, I toured European countries choosing from each the winner of a national beauty competition, whose prize was a part in the film. They titted about the set, draped themselves about pillars in Fu Manchu's great stone den, and between takes some draped themselves about members of the unit. But they could not show themselves off to best advantage because they were not members of Equity and therefore they had not a line to speak between the whole dozen.'

That didn't deter HAT though, who went on to film *The Castle of Fu Manchu* – a Spanish/Italian/West German co-production shot in Turkey – beginning with Fu freezing the Atlantic and wrecking an ocean liner via spliced-in clips from *A Night to Remember*, tinted a spectral blue in an attempt to disguise the fact that they were shot in black and white and the rest of the film is in colour!

On another occasion HAT was in Rio shooting a film with his favoured director, Jess Franco, who had a reputation for shooting very quickly. They were over a week ahead of schedule, with their next shots being of the finale of the Rio Carnival. Faced with putting his cast and crew on paid hiatus to await the annual festivities, HAT decided to write a script called *99 Women* over the weekend and, with his three female leads, director and crew, shot its action and location sequences in five days, before resuming work on the other film. By the time he returned to London he had one complete film and another third of *99 Women* in the can.

There is an anecdote, possibly apocryphal, about how Towers tried to persuade Herbert Lom, another of his favoured leading actors, to join the cast of a new Harry Palmer spy movie, *Bullet to Beijing*, starring Michael Caine.

'It will be shot in Russia in an exciting location where few film crews have ever gone,' said Harry, without naming the place.

When Lom insisted on knowing where it was, Towers replied, after some hesitation, 'Um … Chernobyl.'

HAT had done a deal with Len Deighton to bring his famous spy creation back to the screens, although I believe he had to do a separate deal with Harry Saltzman, as in the first book the spy didn't have a name – that was a creation of the film that Harry Saltzman had produced. So to use the name 'Harry Palmer' didn't have a clear title of use in a new film and necessitated a bit of negotiation.

HAT had found some money in the newly opened-up Russia, tied it up with a Canadian/UK co-production and secured Michael Caine for the lead. Filming in the former Soviet Union meant buying certain friendships and protection. Towers said, 'Russia welcomed us with open palms.'

On another occasion, cameraman Ronnie Maasz told me about joining one of HAT's productions in Salzburg. Rather than pay to shoot in a studio, the prudent producer opted to adapt hotel bedrooms, houses, offices and any other setting he could acquire cheaply, with sets dressed as they went along. The actors were mainly German (as that's where his finance came from) and Ronnie discovered they had actually started the film in Prague, but for 'financial reasons' everything was transported across the border overnight and re-set in Austria.

The first shot was to be of an exotic white sports car, but a rusty old Czech Tatra turned up. HAT declared it only needed a quick re-spray – and he knew just where to get it done. An hour later, the car returned to the set sporting a new paint job that was a curiously flat shade of white. Soon after, it started to rain and the colour washed off the car – he'd had it painted on the cheap and the local painter had used emulsion! Not to be outdone, HAT approached a local shopper and asked if he could borrow his white sports car, to which, amazingly, the local agreed. Unfortunately, though, Harry failed to think ahead to the next day's shooting requirements. So, on day two another white car was found – an entirely different model – and HAT ordered shooting to continue, reasoning, 'No one will notice – they'll be too caught up in the plot!' Needless to say, everyone noticed!

ABOVE: With Tony Curtis and Lord Lew Grade, a formidable producer and a great friend.

✦

One time, filming in Rome, I met for lunch with an old friend of mine. Vincenzo Labella was a lecturer in Vatican History and Art in Florence and Rome, and later became a very successful writer and producer, after starting out as a technical advisor on *Francis of Assisi*. Over lunch, Vincenzo told me his next project as a producer was going to be on the television series *Jesus of Nazareth* for Lew Grade. In fact, it transpired, he was going to the airport that very afternoon to pick Lew up, as they had some meetings to attend about the new series.

It was an opportunity I couldn't resist. I asked Vincenzo if I could act as their chauffeur. I said I would wear a jacket and cap ... all I asked was that Vincenzo went along with anything I said.

'OK,' he said, eyeing me suspiciously.

At the airport, Lew got into the back of the car, puffing on his trademark cigar, and, without looking around, in my best Italian I asked, '*Dove vorresti che guidi?*'

'What? What did he say?' barked Lew.

'Oh,' said Vincenzo, 'he just asked where are we going.'

'What sort of driver is he if he doesn't know where we're going?' Lew snapped.

'It's OK, he's merely confirming ...' said Vincenzo.

I started driving and waited for them to become engrossed in conversation before I interrupted them. '*Mi scusi, signore, ma la prego di chiedere al signore si è alla guida con se posso avere uno dei suoi magnifici sigari?*'

'What? What did he say now?' asked an irritated Lew.

'He wants to know if he can have one of your fine cigars?' said Vincenzo.

'What the bloody hell is going on here?' cried Lew.

I turned around and smiled.

'Stop the car!' he shouted. He got out, went to the boot, pulled out a huge box of Montecristos and gave them to me, laughing his head off. Lew's trademark was his wonderful, large Havana cigar. Comedian Dave Allen always said of him, 'Never wear a brown suit when you're around Lew as he'll pick you up and try to light you.'

Lew was a great friend to me, and although he was of Jewish-Russian extraction, I think he'd have converted to any religion if it meant getting a deal. Kathy, Lady Grade, is Catholic and when she was invited to an audience with the Pope in Rome in the 1970s, Lew naturally travelled with her.

'Roger,' he later told me, 'Pope held Kathy's hand and blessed her, blessed her family and blessed the work of her beloved husband. Then Pope called me over, and do you know what Pope said, Roger? He said, "Mr Grade, I want to bless you for all of the great work you produce and in particular I want to thank you for making *Jesus of Nazareth*."'

'Oh really, Lew?'

'Yes, and do you know what else, Roger? Well, the following Sunday when Pope came out on his balcony to bless the crowds in St Peter's Square ...'

'Yes, Lew?' I asked.

'Well, Roger. That Sunday he held up his hands to bless the crowds and said, "Bless you, my children, and be sure you watch *Jesus of Nazareth* on TV tonight!"'

Lew initially sold the series to NBC in America, and such was its popularity that NBC asked Lew to fly over to negotiate a deal for repeat screening rights. Just before he left he received a call from Proctor & Gamble Entertainment saying that they wanted to buy the show and all future re-run rights with it. It was hot property.

On the plane going over to LA, Lew said he had a vision, 'And that vision was of the number 25.' He knew it wasn't $25 and it couldn't be $25,000, so when he went into his first meeting with the P&G executives he told them the price was $25 million.

They told him he was crazy.

He went to see NBC next, as planned, and they asked how much he wanted. '$25 million,' he beamed.

They only wanted five re-runs and after an hour of negotiating said their top price was $15.5 million – Lew wasn't interested.

His next LA meeting was at CBS, where he was pitching a new mini-series with Sophia Loren and Omar Sharif, but he felt the executives just weren't biting and couldn't figure out why, so he asked them point-blank if he'd done anything to upset them.

'What about offering us repeats of *Jesus of Nazareth*?' they asked.

'NBC have first option to buy it and I want $25 million,' said Lew.

'OK, when do you want to know?' they asked.

'I'm leaving for the airport at 4 p.m.'

'You'll hear from us by then.'

Lew, meanwhile, called back NBC and said they had twenty-eight minutes to reach a decision on buying the show, and the price was $25 million, take it or leave it. It was chutzpah on a grand scale. Ten minutes later, the chairman, Herbert Schlosser, called him. 'Lew, we've been friends for fifteen years. How can you do this to me? I need time.'

'You've got twenty minutes left,' Lew said, 'before I offer it to CBS.'

Sure enough, NBC came up with the $25 million.

When asked later how he arrived at the visionary figure, Lew shook his head and said, 'I don't know, but I couldn't believe they paid it!'

While *Jesus of Nazareth* was a production triumph for Lew's company, ITC, the jewel in his weekly network television schedule was undoubtedly the variety show *Sunday Night at the London Palladium*, and one Sunday Lew made a star out of a puppet act called 'Topo Gigio'. A few months later they were short of a 'top of the bill' act and on the Friday prior to the show word came back to Lew that he was not to worry as they'd secured Tito Gobbi (the famous Italian baritone).

'Aww, no!' cried Lew. 'Not that bloody mouse act again.'

Towards the end of his life, Lew was approached by the chiefs at Polygram Films, who hit the jackpot in 1994 with *Four Weddings and a Funeral,* and who had then recently acquired the ITC library of programmes and films that Lew had green-lit, financed and/or produced – including *The Saint, The Persuaders!, Randall & Hopkirk Deceased, The Baron, The Champions, Raise the Titanic, Escape to Athena* and so on. It was a vast library and had been wrestled from Lew in the 1980s after he lost control of his empire due to some unfortunate business dealings.

Anyhow, the proposition was for Lew to be appointed non-executive chairman of Polygram – a figurehead position more than anything else. They offered him the annual salary of £100,000.

'That's not enough,' said Lew abruptly. 'Make it £150,000.'

The two chiefs, Stewart Till and Michael Kuhn, were a little taken aback as they were effectively offering him a job with little work involved for a not inconsiderable sum of money.

'But, Lew, we can't go any higher! You only have to attend a couple of meetings a year,' they reasoned.

'Well, you boys think about it,' said Lew.

Deflated and somewhat stumped, Till and Kuhn said they'd get back to Lew after their impending trip to Germany, where they hoped to conclude a deal with the huge Kirsch Media TV empire to license some of the ITC shows.

'I'll come with you!' said Lew. 'If I'm going to be chairman I need to earn my £150,000.'

Despite their protests that they had already more or less sewn up the deal and didn't need any help, Lew was insistent.

Arriving at Heathrow airport to board their flight a couple of days later, they saw Lew emerge from his Rolls-Royce and enter the departure hall, trademark cigar firmly in his mouth. The 'no smoking' policy was something completely alien to Lew and consequently something he ignored. His young executive friends wondered what they might be getting themselves into with this larger-than-life character who lived life very much on his terms and who seemed adamant that lending his name to their already successful company was worth £150,000.

On arriving at Kirsch HQ, Lew was immediately whisked up to see Leo Kirsch, the head of the company, and launched straight into Yiddish with his old friend. They swiftly disappeared, arm-in-arm, into an office, while Kuhn and Till were left outside worrying that their long-gestating deal was about to be blown. A few minutes later, Lew emerged.

'OK, boys. The deal is done,' he told them. 'Let's go for lunch.'

Kuhn and Till, by now rather furious, told Lew he had no right to interfere with their negotiations and that he didn't even know how much they'd bargained on getting, so had undoubtedly sold them short.

'How much did you want?' asked Lew.

'We were edging towards £200,000,' said 'the boys'.

'I just got you £300,000, boys,' Lew smiled. 'Now you see why I'm worth that extra fifty?'

Needless to say, Lew became their chairman at his proposed fee.

There was much talk of remaking some of the classic TV shows, and I know Lew was very keen to revisit his past successes and took to the chat show sofas to talk about it all. Sadly, Lew passed away before many of his plans could come to fruition. Soon after, Polygram hit financial problems and the company's Dutch parent company announced it was withdrawing from film production, selling its catalogue to ITV.

Lew's brother, Lord Bernard Delfont – or Bernie to his friends – was also very active in film finance and production and was, in fact, the person who invited my old friend Bryan Forbes to head up ABPC's production activity in the late 1960s. Later on, in 1978, Bernie, as chairman of the now renamed EMI Films, had backed a little British film called *The Life of Brian*, which was the brainchild of the Monty Python team.

Bernie was set on investing a great deal of his company's money in the movie but at the last minute got cold feet about the religious subject matter – and not least about the image of 'Brian' on a crucifix singing, 'Always look on the bright side of life.' Bernie pulled out just days before shooting was due to start.

Faced with finding another backer at short notice, the team were all set to throw in the towel when Eric Idle suddenly remembered a chap he recently met at a party – former Beatle George Harrison. Not having time to beat about the bush, Idle came straight to the point and asked Harrison if he would be interested in bailing out the film for $4 million. Harrison read the script the following day, loved it immediately, and agreed to come on board. Idle later described this moment as 'the most expensive movie ticket ever purchased'. Harrison formed Handmade Films with his business manager Denis O'Brien and production commenced.

The film was an enormous success and although Handmade was formed originally to produce only one film, they soon found themselves becoming involved with another when the gangster movie *The Long Good Friday* came their way. The film had been completed but its production company, Black Lion Films, which was owned by Lew Grade, was becoming nervous about its prospects due to the high level of violence and a key subplot involving the IRA. Handmade made an offer to buy the rights for £700,000 and released the film, which proved to be another huge hit.

Harrison once said, 'As a musician I've been the person who's said of the people with the money, "What do they know?" and now I'm that person. But I know that unless you give an artist as much freedom as possible, there's no point in using that artist.'

The company continued producing movies into the early 1990s when it was sold, though, alas, they never gave me a job!

Another important producer in my life, and indeed in the movie business as a whole, was Harry Saltzman. The often brash, frequently loud and always extravagant producer was actually Canadian, born in Quebec, and not American as many people incorrectly assumed.

I know Harry didn't have a particularly happy childhood and ran away from home aged fifteen to join the circus. Such was his entrepreneurial spirit, two years later he was running his own circus troupe.

During the 1940s he joined the army, serving in World War II, where he was posted to Paris and was later recruited to the OSS – the Office of Strategic Services, an intelligence division. Such was the sensitivity of his work that when in 2003 his daughter Hilary wanted to move to Quebec from LA, she had to prove her father was a Canadian citizen, so contacted the Department of State to retrieve Harry's records. Those relating to his military service were said to need the permission of the Secretary of State himself before they could be released, and even then they were edited heavily – some sixty years after the fact.

After the war, Harry stayed on in Paris where he met Jacqueline, a Romanian who had escaped from the troubles of her homeland, and they married soon after. In Paris he found work as a casting agent but despite modest success he never really made his mark in the profession, nor a great deal of money. He next became involved in a TV series about the French Foreign Legion, which proved more profitable and, after joining British producer Betty Box to work on *The Iron Petticoat*, Harry realized that there were more rewarding opportunities in the film business and, together with Tony Richardson and John Osborne, he formed a production company with the hopes of being able to find finance for more features. They called the collaboration Woodfall Productions and Harry finally found his real vocation in life.

Look Back in Anger cast rising Welsh actor Richard Burton as the lead, and Harry sought out various other stage plays

ABOVE: Harry Saltzman (*left*) and Cubby Broccoli (*right*) with the man who created James Bond, Ian Fleming.

he thought fitting for the screen. *Saturday Night and Sunday Morning* followed in 1960, starring a young Albert Finney. When the James Cagney film *The Gallant Hours* opened in Leicester Square, it did terrible business and was pulled after just three days. The manager, keen to find something else to screen immediately, was offered *Saturday Night* and the rest, as they say, is history ... The film scooped three BAFTA awards, including Best British Film, and made a fortune!

The Entertainer, starring Laurence Olivier, was another award-winning production, but soon after that the Woodfall team parted ways to pursue their own projects. Harry was looking for another investment and turned to a successful series of novels by Ian Fleming. He reportedly paid $50,000 for the rights in 1961, a huge sum for the times, and his pricey offer earned him just a six-month option on the James Bond character. But in teaming with Cubby Broccoli on the eve of expiry of his option, a deal was done with United Artists and Jim Bond hit the big screen.

Jess Conrad told me a great story about when he came across Harry. Jess, who aside from being a big singing star had also made a foray into films, went up for roles in a number of TV commercials but never seemed to get them. It was, he reasoned to his friend and fellow struggling thespian Gareth Hunt, who was experiencing similar problems at the time, because neither of them had blue eyes – all the Paul Newman lookalikes were getting the jobs they went up for. So they decided the best thing to do would be to invest in a pair of blue contact lenses between them. At the time, contact lenses were very expensive and they could only afford one each. They agreed to take it in turns to wear them.

When the call went out to find a new James Bond in 1968, Jess wangled himself an audition and called Gareth Hunt, 'Can I borrow the lens tomorrow?' When Gareth asked why, Jess wanted to throw him off the scent of this juicy role. 'Oh, it's nothing, just a commercial for something or other,' he lied.

So, Jess got the lenses. You must remember that at this time contact lens technology was pretty young, and the only problem with the lenses was that although they *looked* good, you couldn't actually *see* much through them.

Jess duly reported at the production company EON's South Audley Street office and, running a little late, told the receptionist that he had a meeting with Harry Saltzman. He was told to go up to the office so he dashed up the stairs and when he reached the top he realized he hadn't put the lenses in so, a little out of breath and somewhat nervous, he started trying to put the lenses in, only to drop one on the floor. On his hands and knees Jess started feeling through the deep carpet pile for the lens. Eventually he found it and stuck it straight in, knocked on the door and entered.

'The name's Conrad, Jess Conrad,' he stated confidently.

'I'm over here,' replied Harry Saltzman, wondering why this actor was talking to a hat stand.

'Oh, yes,' Jess said, swivelling around.

Unfortunately, the lens had picked up some fluff and grit from the carpet, and as if it wasn't bad enough that he couldn't see much with the lenses in, now tears were running down his cheek thanks to the grit in his eye – not *quite* the persona for a fearless 007.

The interview lasted a few minutes and Jess left, still wearing the lenses, only to miss his footing on the top stair, and fall all the way down. As he clattered to a halt at the bottom, Harry appeared at the top of the stairwell, laughing riotously, and shouted, 'You'll never be James Bond – but I'd love to sign you up as a stunt man!'

Such was the success of the Bond films that Harry and

Cubby began to make more money than they knew what to do with. Guy Hamilton was in Cubby's office one day after *Goldfinger* opened and Harry called through on the

BELOW: I'll always be grateful to Harry and Cubby for giving me the chance to play Jimmy Bond.

speakerphone:'Cubby, I know what we should do with our money. We'll buy gold!'

'But where would we keep it all?' Cubby asked, worriedly.

I had been great friends with Harry from the early 1960s, though that all changed when I started working for him. You see, Harry had this belief that if he paid you, then he owned you. I know he had a contract with Albert Finney, for example, where Albie had to seek his permission to work elsewhere.

When we started *Live and Let Die* his partnership with Cubby was beginning to crack around the edges, and Harry effectively ran the production on the film by agreeing Cubby would do similar on the next – it was a way of minimizing the time they had to spend working together.

Harry loved making movies and made many other non-Bond films, whereas Cubby was content to concentrate on the franchise.

Once I signed as 007, Harry became very possessive and felt he owned me. He demonstrated it, for example, by not allowing my friend David Hedison to stay at the same hotel as me because he was jealous of our friendship. He argued about my long-time hairdresser, Mike Jones, joining the production ... and things like that.

I know director Guy Hamilton felt caught in the middle of the two producers and told UA that he could happily make a film with Harry, and could happily make a film with Cubby, but he wasn't keen on making a film with Cubby and Harry together.

However, for all his faults, Harry was still an amazing showman and he loved making movies.

ABOVE: Another legendary filmmaker and philanthropist, Sir Run Run Shaw. His use of ginseng root tea was thought to have helped keep him going to the ripe age of 106.

Greg Peck once told me about a meeting he had with the producer Run Run Shaw in Hong Kong. Shaw was a tremendously successful film mogul and philanthropist and founded Shaw Brothers Studios, which became one of the best-known film production companies in Hong Kong. Greg had gone over to meet with the great man and see his studio, where they shot all the Kung Fu and karate movies that were so popular all over the Far East. Anyhow, they were sitting in Run Run Shaw's office and Shaw brought out a beautiful, highly polished mahogany box, lined with red velvet, and lying inside was a large, knobbly ginseng root. Run Run Shaw told Greg that this particular piece of ginseng was from the mountains of mainland China, where mountaineers would hunt down the roots and dig them out with small spoons in order to preserve the root intact.

I should add that at this stage, Run Run Shaw was in his early seventies, incredibly rich and very charming.

'Gregory, I take three capsules of this every morning, and three more at night before I go to bed. I have a man grind this root up for me into a powder and I wash it down with a tot of Scotch,' declared the producer. 'And I can still do everything – I mean *everything* – that I could when I was thirty,' he added, leaving Greg in no doubt as to what he meant.

Seeing how well ginseng worked at keeping Run Run Shaw on top form, dear Greg decided that it might just work for his old friend Niv, who had been ailing rather markedly the last time they had met. He duly sent some along to David Niven, but heard shortly after that Niv's doctors, already worried about him, were monitoring all his intake and wouldn't allow him to take it.

There's got to be something in it, though. I remembered that story when I read about Run Run Shaw's death in January 2014 – at the tender age of 106.

❧

Of course, films featuring would-be heroic actors such as me only come about because of the ingenuity, negotiating and charming skills of producers. One who had all that in bucket loads was Elliott Kastner, who was most definitely one of the largest larger-than-life characters in the film business. He had a damn good eye for a commercial story, but then again he did start his career as a literary agent, so he ought to have known a good book when he read one.

I only made one film with Elliott, *North Sea Hijack*, but knew him socially and from around Pinewood, where he kept an office for most of his working life. When he was in residence you'd know because there was no mistaking his voice booming down the corridor when he was on the phone, having rather heated conversations with financiers and executives, which often ended with Elliott lovingly telling them where to 'shove it'.

I think it's fair to say that Elliott was in litigation for most of his life with one person or another, but he also made more films than anyone else I know.

He was always on the lookout for well-heeled people in his never-ending pursuit of what he'd call the 'war chest', and the story goes that whenever Elliott arrived in LA he would stay at a well-known and rather luxurious hotel. On arrival, he would slip a very handsome gratuity to the reservations manager and ask if there were any residents from Texas in the large suites. He'd then go to their rooms, knock on the door and introduce himself. Over the years, Elliott had worked out that they were pretty likely to be wealthy oil executives and he'd always have a script to tell them about and an exciting opportunity for them to be in movies.

A couple of years before we started shooting *North Sea*

Hijack, Elliott had cast Marlon Brando and Jack Nicholson in a movie called *The Missouri Breaks*.

Brando was a great believer in 'the method' school of acting, so launched himself right into his characters, always trying to capture the character's psychological motivation and emotions. In this case he did so by catching grasshoppers in his downtime and eating a live frog. If that wasn't bizarre enough, the Western saw Brando speaking in an over-the-top Irish accent, and wearing a dress too.

When he was trying to pull the finance for the film together, Elliott heard that Jack Nicholson had just moved into a house near Marlon Brando's, and so he courted them both to star. He knew if both men agreed then the finance was assured. Brando was at the peak of his powers and Elliott happily yielded to demands both large and small in order to secure him, including hiring Arthur Penn to direct. But despite satisfying their every demand, neither Brando nor Nicholson would quite commit. So Elliott did the only thing he could – he resorted to subterfuge, telling both of them that the other *had* agreed a deal. Not long after that they both happily signed on the dotted line! That was Elliott.

Postscript

A FEW YEARS AGO, WITH MY BRITISH PASSPORT COMING UP FOR renewal, I thought the easiest and quickest way of picking up a replacement was to book a one-day appointment at the Passport Office in London, where the plan was that I would fill in a form, bring a couple of photos and return after lunch to pick up my new document.

Upon handing my duly completed renewal paperwork to the man behind the counter, he tutted and said my signature was 'outside the box' and told me I'd need to go and fill in another complete form. About ten minutes later I returned, and ensured my signature was now well and truly within the appointed box.

'Are these photos recent ones?' he asked as I handed them over.

'Yes, I had them taken a week ago,' I replied. 'In Switzerland.'

'What?'

'A week ago ...' I repeated.

'You said Switzerland?' he asked, as he dropped them back on the desk. 'I'm afraid we can't accept these, as they are not on approved UK photographic paper.'

I was somewhat taken aback, but my interrogator was not someone I felt I could be in any way glib with, so, looking forlorn, I asked what I could do.

'Down that corridor,' he pointed. 'Turn left and follow it

to the end and you'll see a photo machine there. It costs £5 and will print you four. When you have them, come back.'

After what seemed like a three-mile hike, I managed to obtain the photos, though obviously by then I wasn't in a terribly good mood as I look most perturbed in them. I dropped them back to my friend. He read through the form again, looked at the photos … 'I'm sorry, but this is a different person.'

'Pardon?' I asked.

'On your current passport you are named as *Mr* Roger Moore, but now you want it to be in the name of *Sir* Roger Moore – it's different.'

'Yes, I've been knighted in the meantime.'

'Ah,' he replied. 'Do you have any proof of that?'

'Proof?! What would you like?' I seethed through clenched teeth. 'A letter from the Queen?'

With that, he finished off the paperwork and matter-of-factly told me to report back to the office around the corner in three hours.

Following lunch and a much-needed glass of wine, I reported to what I can only really describe as a hatch in a wall, where I rang the bell and waited for said hatch to open.

'Name?' the little man said.

'Roger Moore.'

'Date of birth?'

'14 October 1927.'

'Got any ID on you?'

It's at times like this I'm incredibly tempted to say 'Do you know who I am?' (Or as in the case of when I was in New York for an interview promoting my first book, and the door security man (who had my name on his list) said,

'I can't let you in without photo ID', I slapped my book down in front of him and said, 'There! That's me and that's my name,' and walked through past him.) On this occasion, though, I think I produced either my driving licence or credit card.

He studied my ID very carefully and held it up against my passport. 'Ah, yes, that's fine.'

I took my passport and just as I was about to turn and exit, the little man called out, 'Excuse me!'

I returned to his hatch, and he smiled widely, 'I've always been a big fan, Sir Roger. Any chance of an autograph?'

⁕

I tell you this small anecdote to highlight the fact that whatever one's fame, whatever one has 'accomplished', whoever one has met and mingled with, wherever one has travelled, there are always times in life that one is brought back to earth with a bump. It's true what they say: 'You can take the boy out of south London, but you can't take south London out of the boy. This particular south London boy has always been very lucky. I've worked with the best and travelled the world, made friends with the great and the good and continue to live life to the full – but it's incidents like the one above that (eventually) make me smile and remember my roots.

In Closing ...

ACTING INTERESTS (AND ATTEMPTS) ASIDE, I AM, OF COURSE, still primarily kept busy as a UNICEF Goodwill Ambassador and I'm always delighted when my passion for UNICEF rubs off on those around me. One of my more recent fundraising projects is *Giving Tales*, which came about when my son Christian and his business partner Klaus Lovgreen discussed the idea of producing an interactive, animated version of Hans Christian Andersen fairy tales. *Giving Tales* is an app available on iPhones, iPads etc (although other tablet devices are available, of course ...), and the plan is for a celebrity to read a Hans Christian Andersen story and, as an ever-continuing project, every year the catalogue is set to grow, generating an on-going royalty for UNICEF. I thought it sounded like a terrific project.

I called on a few friends to see if they might lend their tonsils, and the first to jump on board was the lovely Ewan McGregor. Soon afterwards, Stephen Fry, Joanna Lumley, Joan Collins and Michael Caine all joined me in recording tales. I'll keep you posted!

TOP: Kristina and I visit some of the Kosovar refugees in FYR Macedonia in 1999.
BELOW: On our first visit to Kazakhstan, Kristina and I met children with disabilities and were continually inspired.

ABOVE: At UNICEF HQ with Namibian youth representative Livey Van Wyk and fellow Goodwill Ambassador Whoopi Goldberg, unveiling the winning poster of an international advertising competition to promote the Global Campaign on Children and AIDS.

Kristina and I still travel for UNICEF too, and not long ago we were in Germany for the committee's sixtieth anniversary, with various activities, interviews and recordings to tackle. I'm also now deploying my Twitter account to spread UNICEF news, appeals and share success stories – social media is certainly becoming all-important.

ABOVE: 10 August 2004 in Beijing, China, I greet a girl, as other children and members of the press look on, during the launch of a UNICEF-supported summer camp for children orphaned by AIDS.

But thinking back to my early days as an Ambassador, having been recruited by Audrey Hepburn, I often wondered what drove Audrey's total and tireless devotion to the charity. I only discovered the answer at her funeral, when her son Sean read a poem that Audrey had herself read to her family from her sickbed only a few weeks earlier, on Christmas Eve 1992; it was written by American humorist and writer Sam Levenson for his granddaughter.

I found the words so very poignant that I wrapped up each of my recent theatre appearances with it, and indeed with an announcement that UNICEF collection buckets would be in the foyer on the way out – I've no shame in asking for help to save children's lives, and everyone gave so very generously.

For attractive lips, speak words of kindness.
For lovely eyes, seek out the good in people.
For a slim figure, share your food with the hungry.
For beautiful hair, let a child run his or her fingers through it
*   once a day.*
For poise, walk with the knowledge that you never walk alone.
People, even more than things, have to be restored, renewed,
*   revived, reclaimed and redeemed; never throw out anyone.*
Remember, if you ever need a helping hand, you'll find one at
*   the end of each of your arms.*
As you grow older, you will discover that you have two hands,
*   one for helping yourself, the other for helping others.*

Acknowledgements

I would hereby like to acknowledge the invaluable help of:

Gareth Owen for again sprinkling a little literacy on my work; Michael and Lesley O'Mara; Louise Dixon, my editor; Ron Callow, Claire Cater, Judy Palmer and Katy Parker; Lesley Pollinger and all at Pollinger Ltd; Iris Harwood; the National Motor Museum, Beaulieu; the BBC Written Archive, Caversham, Berkshire; *Cinema Retro* magazine www.cinemaretro.com; Andy Boyle; Doris Spriggs; EON Productions Ltd; Alan Davidson of www.sirrogermoore.com

And for supplying many of the photographs:

Jaz Wiseman, UNICEF and EON Productions; Jenny Hanley; Geraldine Winner.

Picture Credits

Index